Genealogical History of the Allen Family and Some of Their Connections

Frances M. Stoddard

Alpha Editions

This edition published in 2020

ISBN : 9789354027659

Design and Setting By
Alpha Editions
email - alphaedis@gmail.com

DEDICATION.

INTRODUCTION.

FROM my girlhood I have taken a deep interest in my ancestry. When, after my eighteenth birthday, I left school, I hoped to learn much from my dearly loved grandfather (Thomas Allen, Jr.) in regard to the Allen Family and their connections, but the month following my return to his home, he was stricken with paralysis, and his wonderful memory was impaired. Years passed on; I picked up what information I could, but my duties as wife and mother prevented my researches, until the winter of 1873, when I began writing a "Family Record Book," intending to ascertain all I could about my father's and mother's families, and make such notes, that my only child, and her children, might know who their ancestors were, etc. I never had a thought of publishing it. I was only able to work upon it, in my leisure moments, for a year or two, when sickness and death caused me to relinquish my labor. Many of my Allen relatives, knowing what I had done, urged me to go on, and finish my book, and have it published, as they wished copies. For the last year, when my health would permit, I have worked steadily, and now that it is completed, I pray that many may derive pleasure from its perusal. I have been more minute in my descriptions of persons and places than I should have been, if my book had been written for the public generally. F. M. S.

THE ALLEN FAMILY

AND THEIR CONNECTIONS.

GENEALOGY AND PEDIGREE OF THE ALLEN FAMILY OF DALE CASTLE, COUNTY OF PEMBROKE, GREAT BRITAIN AND AMERICA.*

FROM a brass tablet in St. Michael's Church, Pembroke : "To the memory of Joshua Allen, grandfather of the Ven. John Allen, M. A., Archdeacon of Salop, and Vicar of Rees, County Salop : Per bend rompu, argent and sable, six martlets counterchanged."

MEMORANDUM : It is proper here to state, that no mottoes were known or used until during the reign of King Henry III, A. D. 1213, and seldom then.

JOHN ALLEN of Dale Castle of Brindley, County Pembroke, had three sons, named John, William and Thomas His award of coat of arms, in 1664, was for bravery and valorous acts in the wars that prevailed during the reign of Charles II, King of England. Arms : Per bend rompu, argent and sable, six martlets counterchanged. Crest, An eagle with wings extended. Motto, Amicitia sine Fraude.

WILLIAM ALLEN, Lord Mayor of London, England, in 1672. Coat of Arms and Crest the same.

---

* This and the three following articles were written by Lewis Denison Allen, the oldest living member of the Allen Family, born August 10th, 1806.

We fail to find the record of the parentage of Nathaniel
Allen, born in London, England, in 1699. From his use
of the Allen Arms, and other circumstances, he is believed
to have been a lineal descendant of John Allen of Brindley,
County Pembroke; he died at Shrewsbury, Mass., in 1770,
aged 71 years.

THOMAS ALLEN, August 26, 1710-1732.

WILLIAM ALLEN, an officer in the army, was son of
Thomas, 1710. William had a son Joseph, of Dale Castle,
County Pembroke. David, son of William, inherited through
his wife, a large estate. Rev. David Allen, M. A., Rector,
Burton, County Pembroke, February, 1769–. Arms and
Crest the same.

JOHN HENSLEIGH ALLEN, born 1769, represented Pembroke
in Parliament in 1819 to 1826. Married Lord Robert Seymour's daughter; had two sons, John and Joseph. Coat of
Arms, Crest and Motto the same.

ELEANOR, grand-daughter of John Allen, Esq., of Dale
Castle, married in 1776 John Loyd. She was grandmother
of John Phillip Allen, Esq., of Dale Castle. Arms and
Motto the same.

JOSEPH JULIAN ALLEN, of Breton, County Pembroke, was
J. P., in 1799. Arms and Motto the same.

JOHN ALLEN, of Brindley, County Pembroke, had three
sons, John, William and Thomas. William died, 1635, aged
75 years. Arms, Crest and Motto the same.

HENRY SEYMOUR ALLEN, of Cresselly, County Pembroke,
Dale Castle, late of First Life Guards; High Sheriff of
Pembroke, I. J., 1816 to 1847. Successor to his father in
1861. Lineage: John Allen, second son of David Allen,
Esq., of Pembroke, by his wife Anne, sister and heir of John
Langhorn, Member of Parliament; and grandson of William
Allen. John Bartlet Allen, his heir, had many children,
among them John Hensleigh Allen, 1818-1836, and Rev.
Edward, Pastor of Pershkerry, 1824. Arms, Crest and Motto
the same.

LAUNCELOT B. ALLEN, of Dale Castle, County Pembroke, married Caroline in 1813, daughter of Mr. Rouailly; they had two sons, George and Edward. Mr. L. B. Allen married as his second wife, July, 1841, Georgiana Sarah, daughter of Charles Nathaniel Bailey, Esq., by the Lady Sarah, his wife, daughter of George, 4th Earl of Jersey; he had by her a son, Charles, born May, 1842. Arms, Crest and Motto the same. They had many children, of whom Caroline married Rev. Edward Drew. They had many children, and many held high offices.

JOHN HENSLEIGH ALLEN, of Cresselly, County Pembroke, a younger branch of Dale Castle, from Kent. Same Arms.

HERALDRY.

HERALDRY is an organization and device of men, and has existed beyond the memory of man, — almost co-equal with man himself. The remoteness of its origin does not admit of any certain date as to time or place.

A more distinct record of its progress is found in the history of the Crusaders of the Holy Wars, and the Soldiers of the Cross; and its maturity was attained in those extraordinary times of reality and romance of barbarism and civilization — more barbarous than civilized. The feudal lord and his frowning fortress; the mailed knight and his gorgeous tournaments, have long since passed away, and heraldry alone survives, the only existing relic probably of either. Its vitality may, however, be traced to attributes peculiarly its own; ministering largely to the pride of man without deeply drawing upon his purse, and without taxing prudence — conferring honors without imposing any harm.

Heraldry, cherished since the nativity, has flourished in every age, in every country, and under almost every form of government. In England it has been fondly entertained, more so than in other parts of Europe, where armorial bearings were esteemed as a part and parcel of the trappings of royalty. But in England a Coat of Arms has always been the indisputable appendage of a gentleman, and be it inherited or acquired, it is equally honorable and an object of pride and display. If inherited, it is the broad seal under which time testifies to the antiquity of the race and the purity of the object; if acquired, it is the golden talisman which bestows the honors of knighthood.

A similar system prevails on this Continent, only to a greater extent; it rewards merit for every noble and humane act. Badges of distinction or medals are awarded by the Government, as a token of excellence in art or for some meritorious act or object, and as an honor conferred on the possessor of them. The Grand Army of the Republic and the veteran are proud of their badges, as is every American citizen bearing a badge of distinction or medal, for some achievement in his profession, or for some humane act in life.

GENEALOGY.

THE science of Genealogy is becoming more and more important to every citizen as our country advances in population and learning. Our first knowledge of Genealogical History is from the Bible.

It is perhaps safe to say that no country has as many important publications on this subject as England, yet it is a rare thing to find the full Pedigree of any one family; all is fragmentary. The collection of material for the Genealogy and Pedigree of a family going back three or more centuries, requires industry and earnest research, and often the labor of years.

There is much pleasure derived from the perusal of all works on this subject, and no one is insensible to the feelings of pride in a virtuous and honorable parentage. It would be most unjust to instance the wise and good of past generations as examples for the emulation of all but those who inherit their family name and blood; family pride is offensive only when it renders conspicuous the degeneracy of the offspring of the great. A perfect equality of the members of a society can only be a proof of its worthiness, but no civilized community exists in which there are no social distinctions. In many communities these distinctions are arbitrary and hereditary; when they are not, nothing but ability in successive generations can maintain the supremacy of any one family. The former case existed in England and America until the Revolution. The latter is now the condition of the United States, and both conditions must interest the genealogists of our beloved country with its liberal institutions, as both are included in the field of their extensive research.

Our country is a mixture of races; such there was in the beginning of our Government. Honor to those worthy of honor; no leveling of all to a nominal equality; no fetters to those who have the will to rise, no opposition is raised against enterprise; on the contrary, a willing hand is raised for the encouragement of all.

HISTORY.

HISTORY gives us a knowledge of past ages; it presents to our view the revolutions that have taken place in the world; it tells us of the rise and progress of nations, and the downfall of States and Empires; it tends to the improvement of the best faculties of man, and enlightens us with a more expansive view of the hidden treasures of the earth. While it entertains and instructs, it instils a knowledge of facts, which elevates the understanding, and furnishes it with bright examples of the leaders of former days, by which our minds are enlarged.

Much of our early history is derived from tradition; the ancient monuments, inscriptions on marbles and stone, even the mounds of earth, and other sources devised by an unintelligent and barbarous people, contribute to our knowledge.

To Herodotus, who is styled the Father of History, we are indebted for the first written account derived from these sources, near five hundred years before the Christian era. His works include everything he could obtain from the learning of the Persians, Egyptians, and other then known countries of the East.

For our knowledge of the ages of the world before Herodotus, we must chiefly look to the God-given book, the Bible; for our information of the primitive state of society and the progress of man in civilization, can only be derived from this source, so full of interest to every reader of the Scriptures, and of such great importance to mankind.

The history of the Crusades, termed the Holy Wars, are full of interest. The Cross was their badge of distinction. Jerusalem, and the possession of the Sepulchre, with whatever else the wonderful cities of the Holy Land might possess, were the objects of their ambition : thousands of lives were sacrificed, with sufferings untold.

The Crusades gave rise to various orders of Knighthood, and imbued chivalry with religious zeal : although ignorance and gross superstition prevailed so widely, yet out of these Holy Wars, sprang a spirit of enterprise, and at last came a better day.

The period embracing the past three centuries is marked by progress in the arts, sciences, and a more general diffusion of knowledge.

The past century exceeds all others, particularly in the United States. The little germ of learning planted with the landing of the Pilgrims on Plymouth Rock, by the Colony of Massachusetts Bay, by the founding of Harvard College in 1636, at Cambridge, Mass., paved the way for the establishment of the free-school system in her sister Colony of Connecticut. These colonists were possessed of many excellent traits of character ; their enterprise and industry, their love of liberty, their attention to education, their morality and piety, entitle them to the respect and admiration of the world.

The progress of this nation has been unchecked and unparalleled in its advancement in science, arts, and agriculture ; in knowledge, in a respect for law and in a love of liberty ; and it is " an asylum for the oppressed of all nations." Happy, indeed, are the people of America ! The electricity of heaven yields to her philosophers ; and advancing art, and new achievements in her mechanical industries, are the attendant handmaids of her progress.

October 15, 1891.

NATHANIEL ALLEN

AND HIS DESCENDANTS.

RECORD OF CAPT. NATHANIEL ALLEN'S FAMILY.

NATHANIEL ALLEN was a native of London, England. The Allen Coat of Arms has Per bend rompu, argent and sable, six martlets, counterchanged. The Crest is an eagle with the wings elevated. It is beautifully engraved on a massive silver tankard, belonging to Capt. Allen, which is now [1890] owned by a great-great-grandson (Thomas H. C. Allen, of Cincinnati, Ohio).

Nathaniel Allen was Commander of a packet ship, which sailed between London, England, and Boston, New England. All the articles on board his ship, and used on his table, that could conveniently be so, were of solid silver, such as gravy boats, cans (used instead of tumblers), porringers, tea-pot handsomely engraved, sugar dish, cream pitcher, pepper box, punch ladle, knives and forks (first style ever made in silver), spoons, etc. Many of these articles are still in the family. There is a damask table cloth, owned by the writer (a great-great-grand-daughter of Capt. Allen), off of which King George II dined, with his suite, by invitation of Capt. Allen, on board his ship. It has among the figures upon it, Solomon's temple, with guards at the gates, clad in armor. Also two men in armor, with a staff between them, bearing one

cluster of the grapes of Eshcol, and the names of Caleb and
Joshua, spies sent into the Land of Canaan, in plain letters
over them. There are other letters and figures upon the
table cloth, and N. D. A. is marked with silk in one corner,
which are the initials of himself and wife, Dorcas.

Nathaniel Allen was born in London, England, in 1699.
He married, and had two sons, born in London, Nathaniel and
Jolley. I cannot ascertain the name of their mother, or when
she died. He married Dorcas Bowes, of London, for his
second wife, about 1726–7. They had twelve children, two
born in London.

COAT OF ARMS OF THE FAMILY OF BOWES.

Ermine, three bows in pale gu. stringed sable ; on a chief
azure, a swan ar. holding in the beak a dish with a covered
cup in it, between two leopards' heads or. Crest, A demi
leopard rampant, holding a bundle of arrows feathered ar-
headed or, banded vert. Sir Martin Bowes was Lord Mayor
of London, England, in 1545.

Nathaniel and Dorcas (Bowes) Allen, with their sons,
Thomas and Samuel, came to Boston, New England, as early
as 1734. A sister of Capt. Allen, Sarah Mann, came with
them. She was born in London, England, in 1695 ; she died
in Shrewsbury, Mass., September 15th, 1766, aged seventy-
one years, and was buried in the old burying-ground.

I found on Christ Church Record, the baptisms and deaths
of ten of Nathaniel and Dorcas (Bowes) Allen's children, viz. :

1 William, baptized, July 13, 1735, in Christ Church. Married,
   May 1, 1760.
2 Henry Jolley, baptized, May 11, 1737. Died, Aug. 31, 1739.
3 Lewis, baptized at his father's, Aug. 19, 1739. Died, Aug.
   31, 1739.
4 Richard, baptized, Nov. 16, 1740. Died, Feb. 6, 1741.
5 Elizabeth, baptized, Nov. 8, 1741. Died, Aug. 27, 1742.

6 A son, name not given, baptized, Feb. 6, 1743. Died, Sept. 21, 1743.

7 Nathaniel, baptized, Dec. 9, 1744.

8 Sarah, baptized, Oct. 27, 1745.

9 Lewis, baptized, Sept. 29, 1747. Married at Shrewsbury, 1770.

10 Caleb, baptized at home, May 8, 1749. Died in Providence, 1774.

Capt. Allen was a shop-keeper in Boston, some years ; his son Thomas was in business with him in 1749. He moved to Shrewsbury, Mass., in 1757, with his wife Dorcas (Bowes), and I think, Nathaniel, Lewis, Sarah and Caleb. He bought a farm. His tax in 1758, was £3, 13s, 4d. In 1759 his tax was £4, 8s, 9d. Capt. Allen died in Shrewsbury, Mass., November 1st, 1770, aged 71 years, and was buried beside his sister. His widow, Dorcas (Bowes) Allen, moved to Leicester, with her son Lewis, March, 1778 ; died there April, 1779, and was buried in her son's lot, on his place named Mount Pleasant. Lewis died November 7, 1782, and was buried beside her.

NATHANIEL ALLEN'S WILL.

In the name of God, Amen. The 18th Day of Auguſt, Anno Domini, one thouſand, ſeven hundred and ſeventy, I Nathaniel Allen of Shrewſbury, of the County of Worceſter, Merchant, calling to mind the mortality of my body, & knowing that it is appointed for all men once to Die, do make and ordain this my Laſt Will & Teſtament, that is to say, principally, and firſt of all, I give and recommend my Soul into the hands of God, who gave it, and my body I recommend to the Earth, to be buried in decent Chriſtian Burial, at the diſcretion of my Executor, nothing doubting but at the General Reſurrecction, I ſhall receive ye ſame again by the mighty power of God ; and as touching that worldly Eſtate wherewith it hath pleaſed God to bleſs me in this life, I give, demiſe, & diſpoſe of the ſame in the following manner & form.

Imprimiſs. My Will is that all my juſt debts, and Funeral charges be paid, by my Executor here-after named.

Item. I give and bequeath unto Dorcas, my dearly beloved wife, and to her heirs and affigns forever (In Lieu of her right of Dower) one third part of all my Real Eftate, and the whole of my Perfonal Eftate, that is not otherwife difpofed of, by the paying of Legacies here-after bequeathed.

Item. I give and bequeath unto my fon Nathaniel Allen, and to his Heirs and affigns forever, the fum of five fhillings.

Item. I give and bequeath unto my fon Jolly Allen, and to his Heirs and affigns forever, the fum of five fhillings.

Item. I give and bequeath unto my fon Thomas Allen, and to his Heirs and affigns forever, the fum of five fhillings.

Item. I give and bequeath unto the children & Heirs of my fon Samuel, Deceafed, the fum of five fhillings.

Item. I give and bequeath unto my fon William Allen, and to his Heirs and affigns forever, the fum of five fhillings.

Item. I give and bequeath unto my fon Lewis Allen, and to his Heirs and affigns forever, one third part of all my Real Eftate, and one half my wearing Apparel.

Item. I give unto my fon Caleb Allen, and to his Heirs and affigns forever, one third part of all my Real Eftate, and one half my wearing Apparel.

Item. I hereby conftitute, and appoint Dorcas, my well beloved wife, my fole Executrix of this my Laft Will & Teftament; and I do hereby utterly Difallow, Revoke, & Difannul all, & every other former Teftament, Will, Legacies, & Bequefts, executed by me in any way before named, willed & bequeathed. Ratifying & confirming this and no other, to be my Laft Will & Teftament, in which whereof I have hereunto fet my hand and Seal the Day & Year above written.

NATHANIEL ALLEN [seal]

Signed, fealed, publifhed, pronounced, & delivered by the faid Nathaniel Allen, as his Laft Will and Teftament in prefence of us the fubfcribers,

MARSHALL NEWTON,
HENRY BALDWIN,
ARTEMAS WARD.

The Will was Probated at Worcester, November 26th, 1770.

JOHN CHANDLER, *Judge.*

RECORD OF THE FAMILY OF JOLLEY, SECOND SON OF NATHANIEL ALLEN.

Jolley Allen was born in 1718, in London, England. He was married to Eleanor Warren, in 1739, who was born in 1724, in London, England. In 1754, Jolley Allen came to Boston, New England, with his wife, Eleanor (Warren). I found on King's Chapel Records a record of the baptisms of eight of their children. The baptism of their seventh child, Sarah, is not recorded, but her birth was recorded at City Hall. I was told that she married a man named Hurlbut, where, I do not know.

The oldest child of Jolley and Eleanor (Warren) Allen, was baptized Easter Day, April 10th, 1757. Jolley was the name on the Records (but I think he must have had some other name besides), for their sixth child was named Jolley, and the oldest did not die until about ten years later. The sponsors of the first Jolley were Nathaniel Allen, Thomas Pearson, and Sarah Mann. Jolley died at Cape Cod, September 18th, 1776, his father (Jolley Allen) said, "from a broken heart."

Eleanor, the second child of Jolley and Eleanor (Warren) Allen, was born December 1st, 1758; baptized December 10th, 1758. Her sponsors were John Ryan, Elizabeth Butler, and Abigail Winter. After her father went back to London, England, Eleanor went to live with her cousin, Thomas Allen, Jr.; while there, she became engaged to Pardon Tillinghast Taber, only brother of Mrs. Amelia (Taber), wife of Thomas Allen, Jr. She took cold and died in 1779 or 1780, at her cousin's, with quick consumption. She was very lovely.

The third child of Jolley and Eleanor Allen, was Henry Warren, born May 11th, 1760; died in Boston, August 24th, 1762. He was baptized May 23d, 1760. His sponsors were Nathaniel Allen, Thomas Greenough, and Elizabeth Butler.

The fourth child of Jolley and Eleanor (Warren) Allen, Johanna, was born August 12th, 1762; baptized August 22d,

1762. Her sponsors were Thomas Pearson, Mary Butler, and Margaret Vinteno. Johanna died in Boston, March 22d, 1765.

The fifth child was Ann, or Nancy; she was born March 19th, 1765; baptized March 31st, 1765. Her sponsors were Nathaniel Allen, Ann Payson, and Sarah Fenno. She died with consumption in 1782, at her cousin's, Thomas Allen, Jr., on the Mount Pleasant estate, in New London, Connecticut, when only seventeen years old.

The sixth child was Jolley, born December 22d, 1766; baptized January 9th, 1767. His sponsors were Robert Stone, Levi Jennings, and Margaret Vinteno. After his father returned to London, England, Jolley, Jr., lived at his cousin's, Thomas Allen, Jr., for several years, and then went to sea. The first that was heard from him was by a letter from his uncle, William Allen, written in London, England, to his brother, Thomas Allen, Sr., in New London, saying that Jolley called upon him after his father's death; the letter was written in 1786. While away, he married, and in 1800 went to New London, Conn., with his wife and a little four-year-old daughter, Mary (called Polly), and lived there a while; he then moved to New York, and had other children; he went again to sea, and we know nothing more of him, or his family.

The seventh child was Sarah, born October 15th, 1769; there is no record of her baptism, at King's Chapel.

The eighth child was Nathaniel, born October 27th, 1770; baptized in private, October 28th, 1770.

Nathaniel, (baptized in private,) lived with his cousin, Thomas Allen, Jr., from 1778 until he chose to be a mariner. In a letter to his cousin, in 1800, from England, he said he was soon to leave for the West Indies; that he owned both ship and cargo. That was the last heard from him.

The ninth child was Charlotte, who was baptized May 13th, 1772. Her sponsors were John Fleming, Isabella Nevins, and Ann Butler. Her birth was not recorded at City Hall.

I do not know whether Jolley and Eleanor brought any children with them from London, England, but Jolley Allen, in his Manuscript, says he lived with his wife thirty-seven years, and she had seventeen children born and christened; as only nine are recorded in Boston, they must have had eight in London, England. I found no notice of their deaths, either at City Hall, or at King's Chapel, or at Christ Church.

Mrs. Eleanor (Warren) Allen, had only one brother. His name was Henry Warren; he was a small man, not quite five feet in height; he was a shopkeeper at Plymouth, Mass., in 1769.

Jolley Allen owned pew No. 54, in King's Chapel, and a tomb under it. He requested his executors, as soon as the times would permit, to bring his remains to Boston, New England, and bury him (as he says) in the family tomb. (Sabine's History of the Loyalists). I think his wish was not complied with, and that his body still lies under St. John's, Wapping, England, where he was buried. His executors were Sir William Pepperrell, and George Erving, son of Hon. George W. Erving, at one time Minister of the United States at the Court of Spain. The latter found among his father's papers a Manuscript by Jolley Allen, written in London, England, in 1780 or 1781 (there is no date in the document). As his father was dead he presented it to Mr. George Ticknor, who gave it to the Massachusetts Historical Society. I made an application for leave to copy it. The sub-committee to whom the application was referred, thought best to print the Manuscript, and it appeared in Volume sixteen of the Proceedings of the Society, February, 1878. The spelling and capitals were changed (modernized). Thomas H. C. Allen and other members of the Allen Family wished to retain the original spelling and capitals, and decided to re-print it, having first consulted Hon. Samuel A. Green, ex-Mayor, and Librarian of the Historical Society, who very courteously said there was no objection to our doing so. A great-great-grand-nephew of Jolley Allen, Mr. Thomas H. C. Allen, of Cincinnati, paid for publishing the reprint of this Manuscript, and his great-great-grand-niece, Frances M. Stod-

dard, of Boston, Mass., restored the original spelling and capitals, wrote a Preface and a Genealogical Appendix. It was
reprinted in 1883, and was an exact copy. Copies of it were
sent to the Genealogical and Historical Societies, and to the
leading Colleges of the United States.

From this Manuscript I learn, that Jolley, second son of
Nathaniel Allen, came to Boston, New England, in 1754,
where he was a merchant twenty-two years. In 1763, (I do
not know how much earlier) he had a shop or store, "near
the Draw-Bridge, Boston," where he sold "at Wholesale and
Retail cheap for Cash a large assortment of English and
India goods, fit for all Seasons," which he imported from
England. He also had ready-made clothing and shoes, be-
sides London, and Bohea teas, indigo and choice cotton wool.
He advertised very largely in the Boston papers. A copy
of two of his advertisements is published in this Genealogical
History.

His last shop, or store, stood about midway between the
Governor's and the Town House, and almost opposite the
Heart and Crown (T. Fleet's printing office). He had also
two warehouses full of goods.

His Manuscript was entitled "An Account of part of the
sufferings and losses of Jolley Allen, a native of London,
England, who with his family and a considerable property,
went to Boston, New England, to reside, in the year 1754."
He says he "had accumulated many thousand Pounds Sterling" in the space of twenty-two years; and continued there
"until this unhappy Rebellion broke out"; and being a
man firmly attached to his King and country, he sacrificed
all for it.

Jolley Allen says his first trouble grew from the fact that
he bought two chests of tea from Gov. Hutchinson's two
sons, Thomas and Elisha; and because a Committee of the
Town of Boston could prove nothing against him, they
injured his trade, etc. During the blockade Mr. Allen
opened his house, to accommodate the British officers and

others : — "General Gage's two brothers-in-law, Major Kimble, and Captain Kimble, Secretary to Gen. Gage, General Prescott, Lord Barrington's son, General Piggott, Captain Delancy, of the 17th Regiment of Light Dragoons, and Doctor Bruce of the Train Artillery. The gentleman above mentioned lodged with me. The following gentlemen both lodged and boarded with me, viz. : Governor Abbott and his Secretary, General Smith, of the 10th Regiment of Foot, Captain Parsons, of ditto, Colonel Cleveland, of the Train Artillery, Cornet Baggett, of the 17th Regiment of Dragoons, Lieutenant Lindsay, of the 14th Regiment of Foot, Captain Lum, of the 38th Regiment, Captain Duff, now Major of the 40th Regiment, Captain Hubbard and Lady, also Lieutenant Snow and Lady, of the 45th Regiment, Lieutenant Hamilton, of ditto, Captain Craig (wounded), of the 47th Regiment, Surgeon Mallett and his mate, of ditto, Captain Follat (wounded), of the 49th Regiment, Captain Smith and Lady, of the 52d Regiment, Ensign Buckannon, of the 47th Regiment, and Major Moncrief and Lieutenant Moncrief, his son."

Mr. Allen decided to leave Boston with the British fleet, of about eighty sail. Accordingly he hired a sloop, named Sally, and took his wife, children and servants on board with him. The sloop was hired of a man who styled himself Captain Robert Campbell, for fifteen guineas sterling, to carry him, his family and effects, to where the fleet and army went ; it cost him forty-two pounds sterling, all ready cash, to carry his goods to the said vessel, about a quarter of an English mile from his house. On the 14th of March, he and his family lay on board the vessel ; on the 17th were towed down below the Castle by strange sailors ; 19th, towed down to Nantasket Roads, by other strange sailors, and lay there till the 27th of March. At three o'clock in the afternoon sailed under the convoy of Admiral Grafton. Their vessel came in contact with two ships, first with one and then with the other, a portion of the main sail had given way, and the vessel was

in danger of being overset; the pretended Captain did not
know what to do. Mr. Allen gave him all the advice and
assistance in his power, but in the meantime, the fleet had
sailed out of sight.

On the 28th of March the vessel struck upon the bar of
Cape Cod, where they remained an hour or two, when a cart,
with a boat or canoe in it, drawn by ten oxen, took Mr. Allen
and his family, eleven in number, on shore, and he walked
the three miles to the town of Cape Cod and his family rode
in the cart, arriving about ten o'clock in the evening, and
were ordered into a small cottage, not fit for one to live in;
he never saw the vessel again. Several carts were used to
bring his goods on shore, but they stored them and he had
no benefit of them. The cottage was in a leaky condition,
and the family had to lie on the floor, or as Mr. Allen says,
"on the ground." They remained in that situation until the
19th of April, twenty-two days, when his wife died, "wanting
the common necessaries of life, and seeing all her effects
taken from her; she fell a sacrifice to their barbarity, and
expired quite broken-hearted, in the 52d year of her age,
with her seven children round her breathless corpse. She
was a good wife and as tender a mother as children ever
had."

Mr. Allen, with a great deal of trouble and difficulty, had
his wife, Eleanor (Warren) Allen, buried on Sunday, April
22d, in the afternoon, at Cape Cod. He remained after her
death, in that disagreeable cottage with his seven children,
until the 27th of April, not able to assist them with a morsel
of bread. He and his oldest son were taken to Truro, eight
miles distant, and confined in the guard-house eight days,
after which time having nothing to allege against them, they
were sent back to the poor motherless children, still wanting
even bread. Mr. Allen, on the 24th of May, obtained a Pass
to the General Court, from the Selectmen of Provincetown.
The Court was sitting in Watertown, Mass., and he and his
oldest son left the other six children in that deplorable condi-

tion until the 16th of August, 1776. They were insulted in their absence. Among Mr. Allen's effects was a "crimson satin damask bed hanging," which he says cost 'one hundred and fifty pounds sterling, and his children saw people with capesheens [capuchins] and bonnets, and others (that could not get pieces large enough) with shoes made out of it; it had been cut or torn in pieces to distribute.'

Jolley and his son left Watertown the 15th of June; not a morsel of bread could they get, even for money; they slept in the woods one night. On the second day, he says, "through the mercy of God we arrived at Shrewsbury, very hungry. My brother Lewis lived on the farm that my father, Nathaniel Allen, bought about twenty years before, for one thousand pounds sterling." There he and his son remained, separated from the other children, until August, when they arrived at his brother Lewis's. Their brother (name not given) was ordered by the General Court to go with an empty vessel to Cape Cod, and bring the remainder of Jolley Allen's property away with him. The people refused to deliver them to him, and he returned with four feather beds and bedding and his six brothers and sisters. He went again, as I understand, to Cape Cod in September, and died there September 18th, 1776, with (as his father said) a broken heart.

Jolley suffered all sorts of indignities because he was a Loyalist, after his shipwreck, until February 8th, 1777, when his nephew, Thomas Allen, jr., took him (by request of his friends) in a chaise to New London, eighty miles distant. When a child, I have heard my grandfather (his nephew) describe that journey. He said his Uncle Jolley was over six feet in height, a very handsome man with dark eyes; very dignified and noble-looking; at every place they stopped he attracted attention. Many questions were asked and he was watched as a spy. They both were happy when they reached New London, for they had to stop over night on the way.

On the 10th of February, Capt. Pardon Tillinghast Taber, Capt. Thomas Wilson and Samuel Taber, carried him in a small boat to the frigate Amazon, lying off Fisher's Island, commanded by Capt. Jacobson, who loaded them with kindnesses, and they staid so long on board that they were seen and recognized, and on their return were taken and imprisoned. On the 18th of February he went on board a ship-of-war; General Robinson received him kindly, and they sailed from Sandy Hook on the 19th and arrived in England the 19th of March, and in London the next day, March 20th, 1777. He found his wife's sister, with whom he had expected to reside, "in Bedlam, raving mad, chained down," she thinking that Mr. Allen, his wife and their seven children had all fallen a sacrifice to the barbarity of the Americans. He was much grieved to find her in such a condition. When he wrote his Manuscript, she was out of "Bedlam" and much better than could have been expected. All who are interested in the life and sufferings of Jolley Allen, should read his thrilling story in his Manuscript; copies of it, as already mentioned, are in many Genealogical and other libraries.

FOLLOWING IS THE COPY OF TWO ADVERTISEMENTS.

DECEMBER 9th, 1763.

Imported from London, to be sold by Wholesale or Retail, cheap for Cash, or short Credit,

BY JOLLEY ALLEN,

At his Shop near the Draw-Bridge Boston. A large assortment of English, and India Goods fit for all seasons. Also ready made Clothing, Womens Cardinals, Meclenburg Tippets, for women and children, new fashion Fillets for young Misses, and the newest fashion Trimmings for Ladies Gowns and Sacks. Women's Calimanco Shoes, of all sizes, and colours, made by the neatest workmen in Lynn, at 38 shillings per pair, and cheaper by the quantity. The very best Hyson Tea at 2 pounds, per pound, and the very best Bohea at 47 shillings, by the Dozen, or half Dozen, or 52 shillings, 6 pence, by the single pound. The best Indigo, per large, or small quantity, very cheap. Choice Cotton Wool 18 shillings (Old Tenor) per pound.

N. B. All the above Teas, and Indigo, are warrented good, and if otherwise, will be taken back, and the Money returned by, the said

JOLLEY ALLEN

BOSTON GAZETTE. September 14th, 1767.

Now ready for Sale at the most reasonable Rate,

By Jolley Allen.

At his Shop almost opposite the Heart and Crown, in Cornhill, Boston. Superfine, middling, and low priced Broad-Cloths, such as scarlet, crimson, black, claret, blue, and cloth-coloured, as low as 33 shillings, Old Tenor per yard. Superfine, middling, and low priced Kerseys, of various colours ; with a large assortment of Krapt beaver coating ; both beavers, and coat bindings. Superfine London, German Serges of most colours, at 36 shillings, O. T. per yard, and some at 33 shillings. Bear skins of different colours. Red and blue diffils, and shags. Plain and silk ragathys, and duroys of the newest and most fashionable colours, very cheap. Neat Damascus Nankeens for Mens Jackets. Black, and cloth-coloured cotton Velvets. Mens and womens black silk Velvets. Rich black Satins for mens Jackets, and white ditto. Worsted plush, and hair Shag, of different colours. Velvet Shapes for Jackets, plain and figured everlasting drawboys. Thickset and fustians of all colours, and prices, with black, scarlet, and crimson worsted thicksets. London and Bristol Shalloons, Tammis, Durants, and Calimancos of all prices and colours. Blue, green and cloth-coloured half thicks. Scarlet, crimson, pink, red and green Baizes, of a yard, and two yards wide, and Flannels. Striped and plain Swanskins of all prices. Osnaburgs, Dowlas, and Tichlinburgs, Blankets of all sorts. Mens, womens and childrens, cotton, thread and worsted Hose. Mens Yarn Stockings. Single and double, cotton Kilmarnock Caps. Scarlet, crimson and striped worsted Caps.

Buckram and stay trimmings of all sorts. Coloured threads of all kinds. Best silk twist. Silk and hair, Mohair and sewing silks of all colours. Best double washed Buttons, some of them new fashioned, white and yellow common ditto. Death-head, basket, needleworked, horn, and horse hair Buttons, of all colours. Horn and Ivory Combs, Pen-Knives, Razors, Scissors, Thimbles, Ink-Pots, Shoe, Knee and Stock Buckles, Snuff Boxes, Sleeve Buttons, Pins and Needles, of all sorts, Writing Paper, Quills, Ink-Powder, Sealing Wax and Wafers. Wide and narrow Lute Strings, very good, which will be sold at a very low rate. Light and dark ground Calicoes and patches, some very low priced. Mens Silk Caps. Striped Cottons and Bengals. Half yard and yard wide Poplins and Crapes. Worsted Damask Grograms and Brocatells. Best Camlets, double, and twisted both ways. Low priced, yard wide Stuffs. Green, cloth-coloured and striped Camleteens. Yellow Canvas and marking ditto, with Crewels and worsteds of all shades and colours. English and Scotch Bedticks and plaids. White, figured and plain Fustians, and Dimithys, 3-4, 7-8 and yard wide Garlix. Large assortment of Irish Linens, all widths and prices. A large assortment of Scotch and Manchester Checks, some Apron width. Mens long black silk Handkerchiefs. Linen and cotton Handkerchiefs, some very large. Knit Patterns for Jackets and Breeches. Silk Knee Straps. Long silk and worsted Money Purses. Diaper, Russia Linen, Tablecloths, &c. All sorts of Garlix and Cambric Thread. A large assortment of silver and other Ribbons, low priced, with necklaces, ear-rings, pendants, head flowers and solitaires. Rich crimson, green, white, blue and black sprigged Satins and Sarcenets, to be sold near the sterling cost. A large assortment of Capushine Silks of the above colours, some black, as low as 30 shillings, O. T. per yard.

Large and small English, and India, romal Handkerchiefs, by the dozen or single. Plain, and flowered gauze Handkerchiefs, and Barcelona Handkerchiefs. A large and fresh assortment of cloth-coloured trimmings, for Ladies Gowns and Sacks. Wide and narrow common Persians. Black, white, pink, blue, and crimson ditto. Pealing Satins of various colours. English and India, black and coloured Taffeties, Taffeta Persians, and plain Persians. Snail Lace and Gimp of all colours. Women's silk Gloves, and Mitts, some extraordinarily good. Men, women and children's worsted, kid and lamb Gloves and mitts. White and black, blond trolly, bone Lace and lappet Lace. Scarlet and white, blue and white, and crimson and white Lace. Plain and flowered Gauze. Paris net and catgut. Leather mount, ivory stick, paddle stick, and bone stick Fans. Children's, ditto. A large assortment of Cambrics and Lawns, some yard wide, and flowered Lawns. Broad and narrow Binding. Linen and diaper Tape. Silk, cotton, and thread Laces, and silk Ferrets. A large assortment Calimancoes, half yard, and half quarter wide, very good at 12 shillings, O. T. per yard. Women's English flowered and plain russet Shoes, of several colours, and very good at a Dollar a pair. Women's Lynn made callimanco Shoes, at 32 shillings and some at 30 shillings, O. T. a pair. Children's best made English morocco leather Pumps. Women's English everlasting Shoes. Women's black and coloured Hats and Bonnets. Women's Chip Hats and Bonnets, &c., &c.

Likewise, Mace, Cinnamon, Cloves, Nutmegs, Allspice, Race and ground Ginger, Pepper, Chocolate, Coffee, Rice, Raisins, Currants, and best English Mustard. English Loaf Sugar, by the hundred, or single Loaf, at 7 shillings, O. T. by the single pound and cheaper by the quantity. Very good Loaf Sugar made here, by the hundred, or single Loaf, at six shillings, six pence, per single pound, and cheaper by the quantity.

☞ Choice Jamaica, and other Brown Sugars, by the Barrel, Hundred, or smaller quantity, some as low as 3 shillings, per single pound, and cheaper by the quantity.

India China. Neat blue, and white China, long Dishes, various sizes, enamelled Plates, blue and white ditto, enamelled Punch Bowls, blue and white ditto of various sizes, enamelled Cups and Saucers, burnt in ditto, with blue and white China Cups and Saucers. Glass, Delph and Stone Ware, both flowered and plain, such as Decanters, Beakers, Cruets, Salt-cellars, Stone-plates, Cups and Saucers, Cream-Pots, Tea-Pots, Bowls, Mugs, Pickle-Pots, &c., by the crate or smaller quantities.

☞ Cotton Wool, very good, and very cheap. Kippers and Tillocks Snuff. Hard Soap. The best of Poland and common Starch, by the Barrel, Hundred, Dozen or single Pound. Choice French Indigo, by large or small quantities. Excellent London Bohea Tea by the chest, Hundred, Dozen, or half Dozen, or by the single pound, half pound, and quarter pound cheap.

☞ The above Tea is warranted of the best kind, and if it proves otherwise after trying it, will be taken back, and the money returned by the said
JOLLEY ALLEN.

N. B. Tea and Indigo, are articles I am never out of:

☞ My Town and Country customers, may depend upon being supplied with all the above Articles the year round, by Wholesale or Retail, and as cheap in proportion as those which have the prices fixed to them, as I deal for Cash only.

RECORD OF THOMAS, OLDEST CHILD OF NATHANIEL AND DORCAS (BOWES) ALLEN.

Thomas Allen was born in London, England, September 19th, 1728. He came to Boston, New England, in 1734, with his parents, his brother Samuel, and his father's sister, Sarah Mann. In 1749, he is spoken of as a shopkeeper with his father, in Boston. After that time and until 1752, he was for some time in the Island of Madeira, where it is said he made a large fortune. When he returned, he settled in New London, Connecticut, and was a merchant, near Ferry Wharf. In 1770, he commenced the first marine list in that city, and continued it until his death. He was also engaged in commerce and owned sixteen sail of vessels. He was voted into the Boston Marine Society, as a Marine member, March 4th, 1760, and paid £4, 10 shillings, for his Certificate of Membership.

In the Annals of St. James' Church, New London, by Rev.
Robert A. Hallam, D. D., Mr. Allen is spoken of as a man of
substance and extensive business, and for a long time a foremost man in the Episcopal Church. He was a Warden ten
years.

He was the only son of Captain Nathaniel and Dorcas
(Bowes) Allen, who had blue eyes, and although a good-sized
man, was not as tall as his brothers. They were six feet.
There was a full length portrait of Thomas Allen, Sr., dressed
in the old style, knee breeches, with silk stockings, knee and
shoe buckles, a ruffled shirt, ruffles round his wrists, a soft
white hat on his head, a pen between his thumb and fingers.
It was a life-like picture. He looked as if he would speak to
you. This portrait was owned by his great-grandson, Lewis
D. Allen, now in Washington, D. C. It was burned in 1853,
in New London, Conn. The loss is great to his descendants,
for there was no other likeness of him. A portrait of his son
Thomas, and grandson Lewis Allen, was burned at the same
time, but there were other pictures of them.

Thomas Allen married, October 29, 1753, the widow of
John Shackmaple, Jr., who died in 1743 ; she was the daughter of Richard and Elizabeth (Saltonstall) Christophers, and
grand-daughter of Gov. Gurdon and Jerusha (Richards) Saltonstall. Elizabeth (Christophers, Shackmaple) Allen, was born
in New London, Conn., September 13, 1714 ; she died August
5, 1783, aged 68 years, 11 months, and 8 days. She had five
children by her first husband. [See pages 30–31.]

Thomas Allen and Elizabeth (Christophers, Shackmaple)
had only one son who lived. He was born in the Shackmaple
House on Bradley Street, New London, September 10, 1755.
He was baptized Thomas by Rev. Matthew Graves, who was
Rector of St. James' Church from April 11, 1748, for thirty
years.

Thomas, Jr., married Amelia Taber, April 23, 1778. He
died in Pomfret, Conn., Tuesday afternoon, May 16, 1842,
aged 86 years, 8 months and 3 days ; his remains were carried

to New London and buried in his daughter's lot, in Cedar Grove Cemetery.

Thomas Allen, Sen., married a second time July 7, 1784; his wife was the widow of his brother, Lewis Allen. Her maiden name was Mary Adams. Her father resided in Worcester. Her brother was Jonathan Adams, of Shrewsbury, Mass. They had no children. Thomas Allen, Sen., died in New London, Conn., November 19, 1793, aged 65 years and 2 months; he was interred in the "Second burying ground." His grand-daughters, Elizabeth Allen and Frances Taber Smith, bought a lot in Cedar Grove Cemetery, April 9, 1853, and removed his remains to that place.

ARMS OF THE SALTONSTALL FAMILY.

Or, a bend between two eagles, displayed sable. Crest, out of a ducal coronet, or, a pelican's head vulning its breast.

The name of Saltonstall is derived from Saltonstall in the Wapentake. Gurdon Saltonstall, Esq., was born in Haverhill, Massachusetts, March 27, 1666. His name Gurdon was derived from the family of his grandmother Meriel Gurdon. He graduated at Harvard College in 1684. His father, Nathaniel Saltonstall, was born in Ipswich, April 9, 1639; his mother was Elizabeth Ward, born April 7, 1647; she died April 29, 1714. Nathaniel and Elizabeth (Ward) Saltonstall had a daughter named Elizabeth, who married Rev. John Denison. Another daughter, Deborah, married Major Thomas Deane. Nathaniel graduated at Harvard College in 1659. He was the son of Richard, who was born at Woodsome, Yorkshire, in 1610, and died at Hulme, England, April 29, 1694; he was the son of Sir Richard, who was born in Halifax, England, in 1586; died in 1658; and who came to America in 1630, in the same ship with Gov. Winthrop, of Massachusetts. He was Ambassador from England to Holland in 1644; and nephew of Richard, Lord Mayor of London in 1597. Sir Richard was the son of Samuel, and grandson of Gilbert, Esq., of Halifax, Yorkshire. Gurdon

Saltonstall had three wives: first, Jerusha, daughter of James
Richards and his wife Sarah, daughter of William Gibbons,
Esq., of Hartford, Connecticut. Mr. Richards died June 29,
1680 ; he gave his daughter Jerusha all his lands and build-
ings in and around New London, Conn. She died in Boston,
July 25, 1697.

The children of Gov. Gurdon and Jerusha (Richards) Saltonstall, were

1 Elizabeth, born May 11, 1690 ; married Richard Christophers
    Aug. 14, 1710, and died 1736. [See below.]

2 Mary, born February 15, 1692 ; married Jeremiah Miller, a
    graduate of Yale College in 1709. He died 1761.

3 Sarah, born April 8, 1694; married John Gardiner, who died
    January 15, 1725 ; her second husband was Samuel Davis ;
    and her third was Thomas Davis.

4 Jerusha, born July 3, 1695 ; died Sept. 12, 1695.

Elizabeth, the eldest daughter, married Richard Christophers,
who was born in New London, Conn., Aug. 18, 1685. He was
son of Richard and Lucretia (Bradley) Christophers. His
father left a large estate. Richard was one of the Assistant
Judges in the Superior Court, held in New London for the
first time, September, 1711. He died in 1736. His widow
married Isaac Ledyard, Merchant.

The children of Richard and Elizabeth (Saltonstall) Christophers were :

1 Richard, born July 29, 1712 ; married Mary, daughter of the
    fourth John Picket. She died Sept. 28, 1736. Their
    daughter Elizabeth, born December 24, 1735, married Capt.
    Joseph Hurlbut. Elizabeth (Christophers) Hurlbut died
    March 11, 1798.

2 Elizabeth, born September 13, 1714.

Elizabeth Christophers married John Shackmaple in 1731-2.
He died in 1743. He was the son of John Shackmaple, an
Englishman, who was commissioned by Robert Quarry, Sur-

veyor general, to be Collector, Surveyor, and Searcher, for Connecticut. The office of Surveyor and Searcher was afterward separated from that of Collector, and the appointment given to John Shackmaple, Jr, in 1728, by James Stevens, Surveyor general. Mrs. Shackmaple, Senior, is supposed to have died about 1730. His son succeeded him in the Collectorship.

The children of John and Elizabeth (Christophers) Shackmaple, were :

1 Sarah, born Wednesday, July 4, 1733, at New London.
2 Elizabeth, born Thursday, Dec. 5, 1734; she married Thomas Wilson, Senior ; they had three children.
3 Lydia, born Wednesday, July 2, 1736.
4 John, born Thursday, May 11, 1738 ; died 1767, and with him the male line of Shackmaple became extinct.
5 Richard, born Friday, July 17, 1741.

Elizabeth (Christophers), widow of John Shackmaple, Jr., married October 29, 1753, Thomas Allen, son of Nathaniel and Dorcas (Bowes) Allen. They had one son, named Thomas, who was born in New London, Sept. 10, 1755 ; baptized in St. James' Church, New London, Conn. His half sister, Elizabeth, (daughter of John Shackmaple, Jr., and his wife Elizabeth Christophers Shackmaple,) married Thomas Wilson, Senior, and had three children :

1 Sarah, who married Robert Colfax, and had two children Robert and Harriet.
2 Elizabeth, who married Jonathan Colfax (brother of Robert), and had one child, named Elizabeth. Sarah (Wilson), wife of Robert Colfax, died, and Jonathan, husband of Elizabeth, also died, and Robert married Elizabeth.
3 Thomas.

Thomas Wilson married Sarah Durfee, and had two children, Maria and Charlotte ; Charlotte married James Edgerton, and their daughter Sarah married Edward Learned, and had a

daughter, Elizabeth, who (I believe) never married. Thomas
Wilson, Jr., after the death of Sarah Durfee, married her sister
Phebe. They had four children, Sally, Elizabeth, Louis, and
Thomas. Sarah and Phebe Durfee were sisters of Richard
who married Sarah, daughter of Andrew Palmer, a graduate of
Harvard in 1703. Andrew was baptized October 1, 1682.

Gov. Gurdon Saltonstall's second wife was Elizabeth Rosewell, only child of William Rosewell, of Branford, Connecticut.
She died in New London, Conn., September 12, 1710, the
same day with her fifth child, Richard, born Sept. 1, 1710.
They (mother and child) were laid to rest in the Saltonstall
tomb, in New London.

The children of Gurdon and Elizabeth (Rosewell) Saltonstall were:

1 Rosewell, born January 19, 1701-2.
2 Katharine, born June 9, 1704; married John Richards.
3 Nathaniel, born July 1, 1707; married Lucretia Arnold, in
   1733.
4 Gurdon, born December 22, 1708.
5 Richard, born Sept. 1, 1710; died Sept. 12, 1710.

Rosewell married a daughter of John Haynes, of Hartford,
Conn., and relict of Elisha Lord. His residence was in
Branford, the home of his maternal ancestors, but he died in
New London (while on a visit to his brother Gurdon), Oct. 1,
1738. Capt. Saltonstall was buried in the Family tomb.
His widow married Rev. Thomas Clap, of Windham, Conn.,
afterwards President of Yale College.

Gurdon, Jr., married Rebecca Winthrop in 1733; their
daughter Rebecca married David Mumford; another daughter
married Thomas Mumford; their son, Winthrop Saltonstall,
married Ann, daughter of Hon. Joseph Wanton, of Newport,
Rhode Island, April 17, 1763.

Gurdon Saltonstall, Jr., was promoted to the rank of
Colonel, April 24, 1740, and to the rank of Brigadier General in 1776. Gen. Gurdon was the first Collector of Cus-

toms under the State authority. He died in Norwich, Conn., at his son-in-law's, Sept. 19, 1785.

The Governor's third wife was Mary, daughter of William Whittingham, and widow of William Clarke, of Boston, Massachusetts. They had no children. She survived him, and died in Boston in 1729.

Gurdon Saltonstall was made Governor of the Colony of Connecticut in 1708; he held the office until September 20, 1724, when he died suddenly of apoplexy, having been apparently in full health on the preceding day. He was interred on the 22d, with all the civic and military honors the Town could give. Colonel Whiting, and Captains Latimer and Christophers, were the officers in command. "The Horse and Foot marched in four files; the drums, colors, trumpets, halberts, and hilts of swords were covered with black, and twenty cannon fired at half a minute's distance." "After the body had been laid in its last resting-place, two volleys were discharged from the fort, and then the military companies, first the troop, afterward the foot, marching in single file, as each respectively came against the tomb, discharged, and so drew up orderly into a body as before, and dismissed."

The Tablet which surmounts the tomb is adorned with the family hatchment, and has the following inscription:—

"Here lyeth the body of the Honourable Gurdon Saltonstall, Esquire, Governor of Connecticut, who died September the 20th in the 59th year of his age, 1724."

While Gurdon Saltonstall was Governor, he used on a Sunday morning to go through his back gate into an orchard and thence to the Meeting-house, moving with a slow, majestic step, accompanied by his wife and followed by his four sons and four daughters marshalled in order, the family servants in the rear.

He was an eminent divine in the Presbyterian Church, and in his office as pastor he was even more distinguished than as Governor.

RECORD OF THE FAMILY OF THOMAS ALLEN, JR.

Thomas Allen, Jr., son of Thomas and Elizabeth (Christophers, Shackmaple) Allen, was born in New London, Conn., September 10, 1755, in what was called the Shackmaple house, afterwards the Wilson house, as his half-sister, Elizabeth Shackmaple, married Thomas Wilson, Sen., and resided in it; it stood on Bradley Street. His mother, as has been mentioned above, was the widow of John Shackmaple, Jr.

Thomas was baptized in St. James' Church, New London, Conn., September, 1755, wrapped in a christening blanket (cloth of gold), since owned by his great grand-daughter, the wife of the Rev. George Herbert Patterson, LL.B., whose maiden name was Frances Amelia Bolles, and who was baptized in St. Paul's Church, Boston, Mass., June 29, 1844. The same blanket was wrapped around her also, and it has been used at the baptisms of eight of her children; as well as with eleven of Thomas Allen, Jr.'s children; thus making twenty-one descendants of Thomas at whose baptisms it has been used, and it looks fresh still.

THE TABER FAMILY.

ARMS OF THE TABER FAMILY.

Azure, on a chevron engrailed, between three lion's heads erased, or, as many leopards passant, proper, collared or. Crest, A lion's head or, erased and pierced with a dart.

Thomas Allen, Jr., married Amelia, daughter of Pardon and Elizabeth (Harris) Taber.

Pardon was a son of Philip Taber, who settled in New London in 1720. Pardon was born in Tiverton, Rhode Island, in 1710. He married first, Phebe Westcote, and lived on a farm which his father bought of James Rogers, in Great Neck, New London, Conn. Their children were:

THOMAS ALLEN, JR.

MRS. AMELIA (TABER) ALLEN.

MRS. ELIZABETH (HARRIS) TABER.

PARDON TABER.

1 Phebe, who married John Griffin, of Lyme. He died, and she
   married Col. Marshfield Parsons, October 10, 1793. They
   had no children. Col. Marshfield Parsons was the eldest
   son who married, of the eminent divine Rev. Jonathan
   Parsons, of Lyme, Conn., later of Newburyport, Mass.,
   and his wife Phebe Griswold. He was born February 17,
   1733; his first wife was Lois, daughter of Richard Wait,
   Senior, of Lyme; his second wife was Abigail Marvin (a
   cousin of his first wife; they were descendants of " Lyme's
   Captain," Reinold Marvin); his third wife was Abigail
   Waterman, of Norwich, Conn., who died March 14, 1793,
   and he married Phebe Griffin, as above. He had children
   only by his first wife.
2 Mary, married Thomas, son of Ebenezer Way. They had two
   children, Mary and Elizabeth. Mary never married; she
   was blind for many years.
3 Elizabeth, married Thomas Way. Their daughter Elizabeth
   married George Champlain; they had four children, George,
   Eliza, Samuel and William. Mrs. Champlain and her sister
   Mary were artists.
4 Naomi, daughter of Pardon and Phebe Taber, married ———
   Hurlbut. Their children were, Phebe, who married Mr.
   Jewett, and Lydia, who married Ebenezer Goddard.

Phebe, wife of Pardon Taber, died, and he married second,
Elizabeth, daughter of Thomas Harris. Their children were :

1 Elizabeth, who married Jonathan Starr, 3d, and had six children : Jonathan, Sally, Eliza, Rebecca, Abby, and one who
   died in infancy.
2 Mercy, who died with small pox; a lovely girl.
3 Pardon Tillinghast. He married Amy Colt; they had seven
   children : Henry, Emma, Frances, Jane, Charlotte, Elizabeth, and a second Charlotte, who died when seven years
   old, and is buried in the Allen lot, in Cedar Grove Cemetery, New London, Connecticut
4 Amelia, who married Thomas Allen, Jr.
5 Luanna, who lived but six years.

6 Frances, married Samuel Seabury, M. D., eldest son of Right
Rev. Samuel Seabury, D. D., first Bishop of Connecticut
and Rhode Island. They had no children.

Pardon Taber died October 9, 1803, in the ninety-second
year of his age. His wife, Elizabeth (Harris) Taber, born in
1731, died January 22, 1806, in the seventy-seventh year of
her age, on Fisher's Island, New York, at her daughter's
(Mrs. Amelia, wife of Thomas Allen, Jr.). Pardon and Elizabeth are buried in Cedar Grove Cemetery, in a lot purchased
by their grand-daughters, Elizabeth Allen and Mrs. Frances
Taber (Allen) Smith, where they now rest, with their own
parents, brothers, and sister Amelia Allen.

Thomas Allen, Jr., went in 1777 to Shrewsbury, to visit
his grandmother Dorcas (Bowes) Allen; while there, she
presented him with a ring set with nine diamonds; they were
cut in the old style, (mirror surface) and enameled back; it
was in a silver box. He gave it to Amelia Taber as an
engagement ring. When her oldest daughter Elizabeth was
a young lady, her mother gave it to her, and Elizabeth gave
it to her sister, Mrs. Frances Taber (Allen) Smith, in 1862.
She presented it to her only child, Mrs. Frances Mary (Smith,
Bolles) Stoddard, on her birth-day, July 30, 1862, who wears
it now, 1892.

Thomas Allen, Jr., was married by the Rev. Matthew
Graves, Rector of St. James' Church, New London, Conn.,
April 23, 1778, to Amelia, daughter of Pardon and Elizabeth
(Harris) Taber, who was born in New London, Conn., February 11, 1758. Their "second-day wedding" was kept at his
father's, in the Wheat house, New London, Conn. Thomas
and Amelia commenced housekeeping on his farm, which he
named "The Mount Pleasant Estate." They had twelve
children :—

1 Elizabeth, born at 11 A. M., Saturday, November 20, 1779,
at Mount Pleasant.

The Allen Lot, in Cedar Grove Cemetery, New London, Connecticut.

2 Thomas, born at 5 A. M., Monday, June 18, 1781, at Mount Pleasant.

3 Lewis, born at 12 M., Friday, May 2, 1783, at Mount Pleasant.

4 William, born at 5 A. M., Sunday, March 13, 1785, at Mount Pleasant.

5 Frances Taber, born at 6 A. M., Wednesday, March 21, 1787, at the Goshen house.

6 Samuel Taber, born at 5 A. M., Sunday, October 11, 1789, at Cedar Hall.

7 Nathaniel, born at 6 A. M., Thursday, June 23, 1791, at his grandfather's (Pardon Taber).

8 George, born at 9 A. M., Saturday, September 21, 1793, at Fisher's Island.

9 Amelia, born at 7 P. M., Friday, July 10, 1795, at Fisher's Island.

10 John, born at 8 A. M., Thursday, May 18, 1797, at Fisher's Island.

11 Henry Nelson, born at 6 P. M., Monday, May 27, 1799, at Fisher's Island.

12 Pardon Taber, born at 9 P. M., Monday, July 12, 1802, at Fisher's Island ; died July 16, 1802.

In April, 1793, Thomas Allen, Jr., hired Fisher's Island, New York, of Francis Bay Winthrop, paying for it an annual rent of twenty-six hundred dollars. The island was nine miles in length, and contained five thousand acres. He had twelve families, who were his tenants ; he also had five or six girls, to spin and weave, two dairy women, a cook, and colored boy to help her. They made two sixty-pound cheeses per day. They also made butter. Mr. Allen kept one hundred cows and two thousand sheep ; he bred horses and mules, and raised rye, wheat and oats. He hired a man named William Westcote, to be both teacher and chaplain for his own and his tenants' large families. He was much beloved by all under him ; one man worked for him twenty-eight years, and others nearly as long.

Mr. Allen attended St. James' Church, New London, Conn., with as many of his family as could conveniently accompany him.   They went in his sloop Betsey, on Sundays and Christmas Day.   During the holidays he always invited all his tenants and their families to visit him, provided an excellent dinner and supper for them, and afterwards sent to the aged, sick, and those unable to be present, a liberal portion from the feast.   All looked forward to the Christmas gatherings, for they had a nice time : a dance, and games for the young people occupied the evening, when Jack (the colored boy) played on a violin.   Mr. Allen lived nineteen years on the island.   When he moved away all his tenants also left, as they said they did not wish to live there without him.

Five of Thomas and Amelia Allen's children were born on the island, as has been stated : three, Samuel Taber, Pardon, and the youngest, died and are buried there.

Thomas Allen, Jr., was made justice of the peace while he lived there, and was always called either Squire Allen, or Captain, as he had been to sea, in 1775, as supercargo ; their trade was with the Island of Madeira, where his father made a large fortune.   He was also, I believe, a captain in the militia.

In 1812 Thomas Allen, Jr., moved to Pomfret, Connecticut, with his wife, Amelia Taber Allen, and eight of their children. Thomas and Lewis were married and resided in Groton, Conn. Mr. Allen bought what was called the Nightingale farm, or farms, for there were two, one of five hundred and twenty acres, and the other two hundred and eighty acres, making eight hundred in all.   In 1815, his son William was married to Emily Chandler, and began housekeeping on the small Nightingale farm, where he built a nice house, which is still in good repair.

Thomas and Amelia (Taber) Allen, moved to New London, Conn., in April, 1816, their sons William and John remaining on the farms.   John's health failed and he left, hoping that a sea voyage would benefit him, but never returned.   In 1824 Capt. Allen and his wife, with their daughters, returned to Pomfret.   They attended Trinity Church, Brooklyn, Conn.,

eleven miles from their farm, until 1829, when the Rev. Ezra
B. Kellogg, who was Rector of Trinity, came to Pomfret and
held the first Episcopal services in a school house in the
village. A Parish was organized, called Christ Church, and
Capt. Thomas Allen and Ebenezer Thompson were chosen
Wardens, and very soon a Church was built, Capt. Allen
giving the lumber. From the time of its consecration by the
Right Rev. Thomas Church Brownell, until his death, May
16, 1842, he was one of the Wardens. He had a stroke of
paralysis, Dec. 26, 1834, and never was able to act as such
afterwards, but I think continued to hold the office. When
in health, (as we only had service in the Church every other
Sunday) he was accustomed to read the service for Morning
and Evening Prayer, and catechise the children in his own
house, on the alternate Sunday; all the hired men and women,
with the members of his own family who could not go to
Brooklyn, were present. His wife read a sermon, and it was
a service I shall never forget. Even now I seem to hear his
voice singing from the thirty-fourth Psalm of David (Prayer-
Book Selection No. 29,)

> " Through all the changing scenes of life,
>   In trouble and in joy," etc.

In 1830 Capt. Thomas Allen moved to the smaller Nightingale farm, where his wife Amelia died about 7 o'clock,
Sunday evening, January 14, 1838, aged 79 years, 11 months,
3 days, from dropsy in the chest. Her funeral was attended
from the house the following Wednesday, the Rev. Riverius
Camp, Rector of Trinity Church, Brooklyn, officiating. On
Thursday her remains were taken to New London, and buried
from St. James' Church, the Rev. Robert A. Hallam, D. D.,
reading the service. May 16, 1842, Capt. Thomas Allen
went to join his loved ones in Paradise; his funeral service
was conducted by the Rev. Dr. Hallam, in St. James' Church,
where he was carried by his daughters, as he died in his own
home in Pomfret. He was interred beside his wife and

father; his two sons, and all three daughters and his wife's parents now repose in Cedar Grove Cemetery, New London, in a lot which his daughters, Elizabeth Allen and Mrs. Frances Taber (Allen) Smith bought, and placed their dear ones in, and have themselves been laid beside them.

Elizabeth Allen was never married; she was a devoted daughter, a true friend, and a loving mother to her orphan nephews and nieces; perfectly unselfish, her life was spent in acts of kindness, for she was a sincere Christian. She was baptized in her infancy, and was confirmed by the Right Rev. Abraham Jarvis in 1800, in St. James' Church, New London, Conn.

Amelia, ninth child of Thomas and Amelia (Taber) Allen, also, was never married. She died June 23, 1852, in Pomfret, after a long illness, patiently borne, while ready and willing to depart. She was at first laid in Christ Church burying ground, and afterwards removed by her sisters to their lot in Cedar Grove Cemetery. Amelia was baptized in infancy, and confirmed Aug. 22, 1817, in St. James' Church, New London, Conn., by the Right Rev. John Henry Hobart.

Particulars in regard to the other children of Thomas and Amelia (Taber) Allen are given below, in the order of their birth.

RECORD OF THE FAMILY OF THOMAS, SON OF THOMAS AND AMELIA (TABER) ALLEN.

THOMAS ALLEN, 3d, was born at Mount Pleasant, near New London, Conn., June 18, 1781. He was baptized in infancy, and confirmed by the Right Rev. Abraham Jarvis, in St. James' Church, New London, in 1800. He married at Pequonnoc, Conn., October 16, 1804, Eunice, daughter of Caleb Johnson. He died of dropsy, May 22, 1817, aged 35 years, 11 months and 25 days. He was a great sufferer for many months. He was buried in Cedar Grove Cemetery, New London.

His wife, Eunice (Johnson) Allen, was born April 27, 1790; died at her daughter's (Mrs. E. B. Forbush), in Buffalo, N. Y., June 18, 1861, aged 71 years, 1 month and 12 days. She was left a widow with six children, when she was only 27 years old. She was a kind and amiable woman, a faithful mother, and her children were a blessing to her.

The children of Thomas and Eunice (Johnson) Allen, were :

1 Thomas Johnson, born August 7, 1805. [See below].
2 Caleb Johnson, born March 27, 1807. [See below].
3 Samuel Taber, born July 19, 1809. [See below].
4 Eunice Amelia, born July 28, 1811. [See below].
5 Emily Chandler, born November 1, 1813. [See below].
6 Lucy Johnson, born February 29, 1816. [See below].

Thomas Johnson Allen, eldest son of Thomas and Eunice (Johnson) Allen, was born at Pequonnoc, Conn., August 7, 1805. He married Lucy, daughter of Deacon Manning, of Pomfret, Conn., March 27, 1825. Lucy Manning was born September 24, 1807. She died February 22, 1838, aged 30 years, 7 months and 2 days.

The children of Thomas Johnson and Lucy (Manning) Allen were :

1 Thomas Henry, born May 17, 1829. He was a physician.
2 George Robert, born June 25. 1830. He is married and resides in Montmorenci, South Carolina.
3 Helen, born February 3, 1835 ; died April 3, 1835.
4 Lucy Manning, born February 9, 1838 ; married December 3. 1857 ; died November 3, 1859. She went to reside with her father, Thomas Allen. in Texas ; she married Thomas Thompson, and died in Texas, having had no children.

Thomas Johnson Allen married for his second wife, his brother Samuel Taber Allen's widow ; her maiden name was Matilda Roberts. Thomas J. Allen died in Texas with yellow fever.

Caleb Johnson Allen, second son of Thomas and Eunice (Johnson) Allen, was born in Groton, Conn., March 27, 1807. At an early age he was apprenticed to the trade of a hatter : having arrived at his majority, he shipped in May, 1828, on a whaling voyage in a vessel owned at New London. On his return the following year, he resumed his trade at Norwalk, Conn., and on January 23, 1831, he married Emily, daughter of Stephen Haley, at Mystic, Conn. He then settled in New London, where he carried on business as a hatter.

It was here that he first indulged his decided taste and aptitude for politics so far as to accept public office. In 1836 he was chosen Alderman and Justice of the peace, which latter position he occupied till 1840. In 1837, meanwhile, he was elected a Senator from the seventh senatorial district of his native State, and in 1838 he was appointed by President Van Buren, Postmaster of New London. This latter office he held until removed by President Tyler, in 1841. "An earnest, inflexible Democrat, of the extremest Jacksonian school, it is related that he received propositions from the new administration looking to a conditional retention of his office. His

spirited reply to President Tyler went the rounds of the
Democratic press at the time, and was a most emphatic rejec-
tion of the overture." Removed as Postmaster, however,
Mr. Allen was in the same year elected Mayor of New London. He held the office until 1843, when he resigned to
migrate with his family to Sinclairville, western New York.
The *Buffalo Courier* says, " Died May 4, 1876, at his home in
Sinclairville, Caleb J. Allen, one of the prominent and most
respected citizens in Chautauqua County, New York.

Emily (Haley) wife of Caleb Johnson Allen, was born in
Mystic, Conn., January 30, 1808. She died in Sinclairville,
New York, May 13, 1887, aged 79 years, 3 months and 14
days.

The children of Caleb Johnson and Emily (Haley) Allen,
were :

1 Caleb Johnson, Jr., born December 21, 1831, at New London,
   Conn. ; died July 3, 1836.
2 James Albert, born January 19. 1834. at New London, Conn.
   [See below.]
3 Emily Amelia, born November 27, 1835, at New London, Conn.
   [See below.]
4 Samuel Taber, [2d,] born April 5th, 1838, at New London, Conn.
   [See below.]
5 Caleb Johnson, Jr., [second of the name] born December 6,
   1840, at New London, Conn. ; died January 2, 1864.
6 Mary, born March 11, 1843, at New London, Conn. ; died July
   9, 1857.
7 Ellen Isadore, born May 9, 1845, at Sinclairville, N. Y. ; died
   July 7, 1865.
8 Stephen Haley, born March 19. 1847, at Sinclairville, N. Y.
   [See below.]
9 Frances Elizabeth, born October 15, 1850, at Sinclairville,
   N. Y. ; died October 29, 1860.

James Albert, the eldest son who lived to manhood, of
Caleb Johnson and Emily (Haley) Allen, was born in New

London, Conn., January 19, 1834, and removed with his parents to Sinclairville, Chautauqua County, New York, in 1843. I copy the following from an article in *The Buffalo Express Souvenir* of 1888 :

" Probably no member of the legal profession in this city is better known than James A. Allen. For many years he has enjoyed a large practice, and many of his law suits have served since their determination, as authorities in cases of a like nature. He began the study of the law in the office of Emory F. Warren, late Judge of Chautauqua County, and subsequently in 1852, entered the office of Welsh & Hibbard, on Exchange Street, in this city. He was with them less than a year ; he was in Sinclairville most of the time until within a few months of his admission to the Bar, which took place at the Erie General Term, held in January, 1856. He commenced practice in his profession in Chautauqua County, and remained there five years. While in Chautauqua, he was associated with Hon. Madison Burwell, and Austin Smith, of Westfield, in defence of Martin Battles, a prisoner charged with murder. The trial resulted in a verdict of guilty, but on a writ of error Mr. Allen took the case to the General Term, which, after hearing his argument, reversed the judgment and sentence, and discharged the prisoner.

" Removing to Buffalo in 1861, Mr. Allen was in the year 1868, employed in the St. John's Church litigation. This grew out of a desire of part of that congregation to change the site of the church. The conservative party retained Mr. Allen, and the result was an adjustment which retained the present site.

" During the past 15 years, Mr. Allen's practice has been chiefly in patent cases. He has had several important suits in the Court of Appeals, and in the Supreme Court of the United States. Mr. Allen's business extends through this State, Michigan, Connecticut, and Northern Illinois. A prudent counsellor and a safe guide in legal matters, there are few more successful lawyers than James A. Allen."

He was married in St. John's Church, Buffalo, N. Y., by the Rector, the Rev. Orlando Witherspoon, November 5, 1862, to Jeanie Pauline Mack. Their children were born in Buffalo, New York :

1 Arthur Holbrook, born October 3, 1863 ; died August 30, 1884.
2 William Albert, born March 7, 1866. These two were baptized in St. John's Church, by the Rev. Orlando Witherspoon.
3 Gertrude Emily, born January 12, 1870, was baptized by the Right Rev. Arthur Cleveland Coxe, Bishop of Western New York. Gertrude and her father were confirmed by the Right Rev. A. C. Coxe. Mr. Allen was a vestryman of St. Luke's Church six years, and has been warden six years and was re-elected at Easter, 1891. The Rev. Walter North is now the Rector of the Parish.

Emily Amelia, third child of Caleb Johnson and Emily (Haley) Allen, was born in New London, Conn., November 27, 1835. She married Obed Edson, May 11, 1859, in Sinclairville, New York, where her husband was born February 18, 1832. Their children were all born in Sinclairville, Chautauqua Co., New York :

1 Fanny Allen, born April 28, 1860 ; married October, 1884.
2 John Milton, born September 29, 1861.
3 Samuel Allen, born September 15, 1863 ; died November 16, 1872.
4 Mary Ursula, born September 11, 1865 ; died November 27, 1872.
5 Hannah, born February 15, 1869.
6 Walter Henry, born January 8, 1874.
7 Ellen Emily, born April 21, 1875.

Samuel Taber Allen, [2d,] third son of Caleb Johnson and Emily (Haley) Allen, was born in New London, Conn., April 5, 1838. He married Emma E. Gilpatrick, widow of Captain Marcus L. Gilpatrick, October 7, 1888, in Kansas City, Mo. They reside in Holden, Johnson County, Mo., where he practices law. Captain Samuel Taber Allen was in Company C, 145th Regiment, New York Volunteers, 2d Brigade, First Division of the 12th Army Corps, under Gen. Williams, and also served under Gen. Banks.

Stephen Haley Allen, the youngest son of Caleb Johnson and Emily (Haley) Allen, was born in Sinclairville, Chautauqua County, New York, March 19, 1847. He married Lucina Smith, December 24, 1872. They have four children :

1 Otis.
2 Emily.
3 Nellie.
4 George.

They reside in Pleasanton, Kansas. Stephen Haley Allen is now (1891) District Judge of three counties of the State of Kansas.

We now return to the children of Thomas and Eunice (Johnson) Allen.

Samuel Taber Allen, third son of Thomas and Eunice (Johnson) Allen, was born July 19, 1809; he lived with his grandfather, Thomas Allen, Jr., after his father's death, and then went to Claiborne, Alabama, where he was a clerk to his uncle, Henry Nelson Allen, for several years ; afterwards he was a surveyor of lands in Texas. He married at Viesca, Falls of the Brasos, Texas, Mrs. Matilda McConnell, a daughter of Elisha Roberts, Esq., of Viesca, Falls of the Brasos, Texas. She was the widow of —— McConnell. Mr. Allen died November 3, 1838, aged 29 years, 3 months and 15 days ; he was killed by the Indians while on a surveying expedition.

Samuel Taber and Matilda (Roberts, McConnell) Allen had two children :

1 Thomas Robert, born April 13, 1836.
2 Eunice Amelia, born July, 1838.

Eunice Amelia Allen, eldest daughter of Thomas and Eunice (Johnson) Allen, was born in Groton, Conn., July 28, 1811. She was with her parents in New London, Conn., at the time of her father's death ; after that time she lived with her mother and sisters in Pomfret, Conn., for several years, and then moved to Bozrah, Conn., where she was married to Samuel Willard Ripley, M. D., June 18, 1832. He was a good physician and a man universally beloved by his neighbors, and in his family a kind husband and father. He died February 13, 1838, in Sydney, Fremont County, Iowa His wife, Eunice Amelia (Allen) Ripley, died in the same place, February 12, 1875, aged 63 years, 6 months and 15 days. They had five children : Samuel, Robert, Henry, Emily, and Mary Ripley.

Emily Chandler Allen, second daughter of Thomas and Eunice (Johnson) Allen, was born November 1, 1813. After her father's death, she lived with her mother in Pomfret and Bozrah, Conn., and subsequently moved with her to Sinclairville, New York ; where she was married July 21, 1836, to Eliakim Brooks Forbush, who was born June 29, 1812. Mr. Forbush was practicing law in Sinclairville, Chautauqua County, New York, when he married ; they afterwards removed to Buffalo, N. Y., where he became a Patent Lawyer, and was very successful. His oldest son, Walter Henry, born February 7, 1842, was associated with him in business. In 1867, he went to Washington, D. C., and on his way home, December 18, 1867, on the Lake Shore Road, at Big Sisters Bridge, near Angola, the train was thrown down an embankment, the cars took fire, and he, with many others, was killed. Mr. Forbush was then aged 55 years, 6 months and 11 days. He was a genial and hospitable man.

Emily Chandler (Allen) and Eliakim Brooks Forbush had two children, Walter Henry and Thomas Allen : the latter was born in Buffalo, N. Y., June 15, 1853, and died July 21, 1853. Walter Henry Forbush, the elder son, married February 11, 1863, Pauline Prince, who was born October 23, 1842. They had three children :

1 Charles Prince, born September 10, 1863.
2 Emily Elizabeth, born August 15, 1866.
3 Walter Eliakim, born October 24, 1868.

Walter Henry Forbush was killed at New Hamburg, N. Y., February 6, 1871, a little more than three years after his father, and by a similar accident.

Lucy Johnson Allen, youngest daughter of Thomas and Eunice (Johnson) Allen, was born in New London, Conn., February 29, 1816. She was baptized in her infancy. After her father's death, she lived in Pomfret, Conn., with her mother, and moved from there to Bozrah, Conn., where she was married to Joseph Smith Emery, June 24, 1832. He was Pastor of the Presbyterian Church in Bozrah at that time; he afterwards moved to Chautauqua County, N. Y. They had five children :

1 Joseph ; during the Civil War, he was in the Commissary Department, at Cairo, Ill.
2 Samuel ; he served in the 42d Wisconsin Regiment.
3 Maria.
4 Sophia.
5 Annie, who married Amasa C. Child, of North Woodstock, Conn. They had no children. Amasa C. Child died in San Francisco, Cal., of consumption, at the age of 34.

BEFORE continuing the record of the younger sons and descendants of Thomas and Amelia (Taber) Allen, we return to complete that of the children of Nathaniel and Dorcas (Bowes) Allen. [See page 14, *supra.*]

Samuel Allen, second son of Nathaniel and Dorcas (Bowes) Allen, was born about 1730, in London, England. He came to Boston, New England, in 1734, with his parents, his brother Thomas and his father's sister, Sarah Mann. He married Elizabeth ———. They had four children :

1 Samuel, born April 28, 1754; married July 25, 1784, Elizabeth Carey; the Rev. Stephen Lewis officiating.
2 James, born about 1756.
3 Nathaniel, born about 1758.
4 Elizabeth, born 1760.

Samuel Allen, Sen., died in 1760, at New Providence, Bahama Islands. He was a merchant. His will was probated in Boston, Mass.

William Allen, third son of Nathaniel and Dorcas (Bowes) Allen, was born in Boston ; he was baptized at Christ Church, July 13, 1735. He married in King's Chapel, May 1, 1760, Rebecca Delap, the ceremony being performed by the Rev. Henry Caner, D. D., Rector of that Church. He left his family in New York City, in 1769, and entered His Majesty's (George III) Navy. In 1781, he was Quarter-Master on board the ship Namur (90 guns). His oldest son was a Midshipman on board the same vessel, and as we learn from a letter of that time, was soon to be promoted. William wrote his brother Jolley Allen, in February, 1781, from Spithead, saying he was not well and was anxious for a discharge ; that letter contained the first intelligence concerning him which had been received for twelve years. His brother Thomas received letters from him again in 1782, and in 1786, from

London, England.   I do not know the names of his children, and cannot trace them.

Lewis Allen, second of the name, and ninth son of Nathaniel and Dorcas (Bowes) Allen, was born in Boston, New England, and baptized in Christ Church, September 29, 1747.   He went to Shrewsbury, Mass., in 1757, with his parents.   He married in 1770, Mary Adams, of Worcester, who was a sister of Jonathan Adams, Senior, of Shrewsbury.   They had no children. In March, 1778, Lewis Allen bought an estate in Leicester, Mass., of Joseph Henshaw, of Boston.   The manor house upon it was built by Mr. Henshaw in 1771, from materials brought from Boston, and is now [1891] standing.   Mr. Allen named the place, " The Mount Pleasant Estate," and kept it in fine repair.   He had one hundred and thirty six acres, including some adjacent land, which he previously owned.   He paid two thousand five hundred pounds sterling for the entire property.   There was a small maple grove on the place, and in that, at his request, he was interred.   In April, 1779, his mother, Dorcas (Bowes) Allen, was buried in this lot.   She had lived with him from the time of the death of her husband Nathaniel Allen.   This lot was reserved by his administrators when the estate was sold, but was ploughed up by a man who hired the place.   I have not learned what disposition was made of the remains of those buried in the lot.   The estate was sold in 1783, and his [Lewis Allen's] widow was married July 7, 1784, to his brother, Thomas Allen, Senior, and went to New London, Conn., to reside.   Lewis Allen died in Leicester, November 7, 1782, aged 35 years, 1 month, and 9 days.   There is an engraving of " The Mount Pleasant Estate" in the History of Leicester, by Washburn, and the removal of Lewis Allen by death is spoken of as "a loss to his friends and the public."

We now return to the descendants of the elder branch.

MOUNT PLEASANT ESTATE, LEICESTER, MASSACHUSETTS.
OWNED AND NAMED BY LEWIS ALLEN, SENIOR, IN 1775, AND OCCUPIED BY HIM UNTIL HIS DEATH.

RECORD OF THE FAMILY OF LEWIS, SECOND SON OF THOMAS AND AMELIA (TABER) ALLEN.

LEWIS ALLEN was born near New London, Conn., on his father's estate, called Mount Pleasant, May 2, 1783. In 1793, he moved with his parents to Fisher's Island, N. Y. He was educated at the Episcopal Academy in Cheshire, Conn.; was confirmed in St. James' Church, New London, in 1800, by the Right Rev. Abraham Jarvis, having been baptized in his infancy in New London.

He was married September 18, 1805, by the Rev. Charles Seabury, Rector of St. James' Church, to Mary Denison Smith, eldest daughter of Denison and Waty Smith. Her father, Denison, was a merchant, and the seventh child of Col. Oliver and Mary (Denison) Smith, whose wife Mary was his own cousin and the only child of Jabez and Waty (Burrows) Smith, Oliver and Jabez being brothers. Col. Oliver was an officer in the Continental Army, during the Revolutionary War. He was born April 27, 1738, and died August 11, 1811. His wife, Mary (Denison) Smith, died September 17, 1800; Deacon Jabez died November 10, 1831; his wife Waty (Burrows) Smith, died September 17, 1823; Denison Smith died December 27, 1860, at the age of 91 years and 6 months. His lovely wife Waty, died August 18, 1853, aged 83 years. All were buried in the Smith Lake Cemetery, Pequonnoc.

The children of Lewis and Mary Denison Allen, were:

1 Lewis Denison, born August 13, 1806, at Pequonnoc, (Groton), Conn. [See below.]
2 Mary Smith, born July 7, 1808, on Fisher's Island. [See below.]
3 Frances Elizabeth, born January 21, 1811, on Fisher's Island. [See below.]
4 Harriet Amelia, born September 25, 1813, at Pequonnoc. [See below.]
5 Sarah Ann, born May 4, 1817, at Pequonnoc. [See below.]

6 Frederick Lee, born May 20, 1820, at New London. [See below.]
7 Thomas Humphrey Cushing, born September 21, 1822, at New London. [See below.]
8 Jane Cellina, born June 28, 1824, at New London. [See below.]
9 Eleanor Caroline, born April 29, 1828, at New London. [See below.]
10 Ann Maria, born May 23, 1831, at New London; died September 11, 1832.

Lewis Allen lived several years on Fisher's Island (West End) after his marriage, and had charge of that farm; there were one hundred cows on the Island and he owned fifty of them, and one of the famous sixty pound cheeses was made there.   After he left the Island, he and his brother Thomas had a farm in Pequonnoc (Groton), Conn.   They removed to New London, Conn., and died there.   Lewis Allen died at' his own house on Main St., May 3, 1844, aged 61 years and 1 day.   His wife Mary Denison (Smith) Allen, was born at Pequonnoc, July 20, 1789, and died in New London, October 21, 1854, aged 65 years, 3 months and 1 day.   They were interred in his lot in Cedar Grove Cemetery.   Lewis Allen was a generous, hospitable man, and a favorite with all who knew him.   He was a Freemason and stood high in the Order.

Lewis Denison Allen, Sr., eldest son of Lewis and Mary Denison (Smith) Allen, was born at his grandfather's (Denison Smith), Poplar Place, Pequonnoc, Conn., August 10, 1806. In early life he resided in New London, Conn.   He received an academic education, and subsequently private tuition under Professor Samuel Palmer.   He married, July 24, 1837, Lucretia Isham, a daughter of Jirah and Sarah (Starr) Isham, and a grand-daughter of Jonathan and Elizabeth (Taber) Starr, all of New London, Conn.   The ceremony was performed at her father's, by the Rev. Robert A. Hallam, D. D., Rector of St. James' Church.   They were both baptized in their infancy and were confirmed by the Right Rev. Thomas Church

ON HIS 85TH ANNIVERSARY, A. D. 1891.

Brownell, Bishop of Connecticut, in St. James' Church, New London Lucretia Isham was born in New London, July 24, 1806 ; she died February 4, 1878, aged 71 years, 6 months and 10 days, in Natchez, Miss., and was buried in Bellefontaine Cemetery, St. Louis, Mo., (Lot 1154). The children of Lewis Denison and Lucretia (Isham) Allen, were all baptized in their infancy. Their names were :

1 Lewis Denison, (Jr.,) born Thursday, April 19, 1838, at New London, Conn. [See below.]
2 Jirah Isham, born Friday, December 20, 1839, at Buffalo, N. Y. [See below.]
3 Mary Denison, born Saturday, December 12, 1841, at New London, Conn. [See below.]
4 Henry Nelson, born Thursday, November 16, 1843, at New London, Conn. He died at seven o'clock, P. M., February 10, 1863, aged 19 years, 2 months and 25 days, of "protracted hectic," and debility caused by scrofula in his knee joint. He was buried in the Allen lot, in Bellefontaine Cemetery, St. Louis, Mo.
5 Lucretia Isham, born Saturday, January 24, 1846, at New London, Conn. [See below.]
6 Thomas Cushing, born Sunday, April 16, 1848, at New London, Conn. [See below.]
7 Ansel Cady, born Saturday, May 11, 1850, in New London, Conn. [See below.]

Lewis Denison Allen, Sr., was a merchant in New London, Conn., and afterwards was a banker in St. Louis, Mo., and also an attorney. He was in the Union Army in the Civil War in the field in Tennessee and Mississippi, and served as an Assistant Quartermaster from July, 1861, to January, 1863, when his duty to his sick family caused him to resign. During his long life he has held many positions of honor and trust, in both military and civil life. From his infancy he has been a member and devout worshiper in the Protestant Episcopal Church, often a Warden or Vestryman, and Treasurer; and at this date (1891), is the oldest living member in regular descent of the family of Captain Nathaniel Allen, whose coat of arms is engraved on a massive silver tankard, now owned by his brother (Thomas H. C. Allen). It was brought to America by his great-great-grandfather, Captain Nathaniel Allen, in 1734.

Lewis Denison Allen aided in organizing a Parish of the Episcopal Church at Connersville, Ind., and afterwards in building a Church edifice. The Right Rev. George Upfold, S. T. D., LL. D., was his Bishop, and in his frequent visits stayed at his house, his wife accompanying him. Lewis subsequently moved to Natchez, Miss., and was selected for the first Mayor of Natchez, during the reconstruction after the war, and was in the Council many years.

Lewis Denison Allen, Jr., eldest son of Lewis Denison and Lucretia (Isham) Allen, was born Thursday, April 19, 1838, at New London, Conn., and baptized by the Rector, the Rev. Robert A. Hallam, D. D., in St. James' Church, in that town. He removed with his parents to Buffalo, N. Y., and afterwards to St. Louis, Mo., where he married Jeanie Shurlds Batte (daughter of Benjamin and Jane Batte); the ceremony took place at the Central Presbyterian Church, February 6, 1867, at half-past eight o'clock, P. M. He was in business in St. Louis, Mo , for several years, and then moved to Monroe, La., where he was Mayor of the city and President of the Bank of Monroe. The children of Lewis Denison, Jr. and Jeanie Shurlds (Batte) Allen, were :

1 Benjamin Batte, born on the evening of January 19, 1868, at St. Louis, Mo.
2 Leela Shryock, born March 18, 1871, at St. Louis, Mo.
3 Lewis Frederick, born at one o'clock, P. M., March 15, 1873, at St. Louis, Mo.
4 Josephine, born October 15, 1878, at St. Louis, Mo. ; died November 6, 1878, aged 22 days.

Jirah Isham, second son of Lewis Denison and Lucretia (Isham) Allen, was born Friday, December 20, 1839, at

LEWIS DENISON ALLEN, JR.

JIRAH ISHAM ALLEN.

THOMAS CUSHING ALLEN.

ANSEL CADY ALLEN.

Buffalo, N. Y.; baptized by the Rector, the Rev. William Shelton, D. D., in St. Paul's Church, Buffalo. In 1883 he was Deputy Postmaster and Indian Interpreter, at Crow Agency, Mont. He is now a merchant at Stillwater, Mont.

Mary Denison Allen, eldest daughter of Lewis Denison and Lucretia (Isham) Allen, was born Saturday, December 12, 1841, in New London, Conn.; she was baptized in St. James' Church by the Rector, the Rev. Robert A. Hallam, D. D.; she was married to William B. Parker, on Tuesday Evening, November 29, A. D. 1859, by the Rev. Edward F. Berkeley, D D., Rector of St. George's Church, St. Louis, Mo. She died at Clifton Heights, near Alton, Ill., the residence of her parents, September 29, 1866, aged 24 years, 2 months and 13 days. She was buried in the family lot, in Bellefontaine Cemetery, St. Louis, Mo. The children of Mary Denison (Allen), and William B. Parker, were—

1 Alice Blake, born Wednesday morning, May 15, 1861, in St. Louis, Mo.
2 Louisa Woodward, born Thursday afternoon, September 10, 1863, in St. Louis, Mo.

Alice Blake Parker, elder daughter of William B. and Mary Denison (Allen) Parker, was born May 15, 1861, at St. Louis, Mo. She was married to Warwick M. Cowgill, M. D., October 27, 1886, at the residence of her aunt, Mrs Henry R. Phinney, on Twelfth street, Alton, Ill.; the ceremony was performed by the Rev. Francis M. S. Taylor, Rector of St. Paul's Church. Dr. Cowgill was the son of an Episcopal clergyman, and was born April 3, 1857.

COWGILL-PARKER.

Yesterday morning Dr. W. M. Cowgill, of Paducah, Ky., and Miss Allie B. Parker, niece of Mrs. Phinney, were quietly married at the residence of Mr. H. R. Phinney on Twelfth street. Only the immediate relatives of the family were present, with Mr. Albert Chapman, the groom's 'best man,' from St. Louis. Rev. Mr. Taylor, of St. Paul's Episcopal Church, officiated. After receiving congratulations and good wishes at the conclusion of the ceremony, an elegant collation was served.

The bride, who is tall and striking in appearance, with classical features, and who is a great favorite in social circles here, is a daughter of the late Wm. B. Parker, of St. Louis. The bridegroom is from an old and highly respected family in Kentucky. He is a practicing physician in Paducah. The pleasant parlors of Mrs. Phinney's residence were handsomely decorated with cut flowers, and the elegant display of presents to the bride added lustre to the occasion. There were many articles of silver and an entire set of Sevres ware with bronzes and repousee ornaments, Bohemian and faience wares, and many tokens from loving friends at home and abroad.

Miss Parker was attired in a stylish traveling suit of gray novelty cloth, tailor made, with cord and passementerie ornaments of navy blue, a jacket of the same and dark blue velvet hat completed the costume.

Dr. and Mrs. Cowgill left on the noon train for St. Louis, where they will take one of the Anchor Line Steamers for New Orleans. They will make their home for the winter at one of the principal hotels of Paducah. Those relatives who came from abroad were : Mrs. D. B. Parker and Miss Lulu Parker, Mr. and Mrs. Henry Miner and Miss Annie Miner, of Winchester, Ill.; Miss Fannie Brown and Messrs. A. C. Allen and Albert Chapman, of St. Louis.

Warwick M. Cowgill and Alice Blake (Parker) Cowgill, have one child, Allen Parker, born July 17, 1890, in Paducah, Kentucky. He was baptized by the Rev. Horace B. Goodyear, on Tuesday, October 7, 1890, soon after 3 P. M., at the home of Mr. Henry R. Phinney, Alton, Ill. The font was beautifully decorated with vines and flowers. The sponsors were Lewis Denison Allen (great grandfather) and Mary Allen Phinney, and his parents.

Lucretia Isham Allen, second daughter of Lewis Denison and Lucretia (Isham) Allen, was born January 24, 1846, in New London, Conn.; she was baptized in St. James' Church by the Rector, the Rev. Robert A. Hallam, D. D. She married Henry R. Phinney, who was born Oct. 7, 1846, in Alton, Ill. They were married by the Rev. Dr. Abbott, in St. Paul's Church, (of which he was Rector) Thursday, November 19, 1867, at eleven o'clock, A. M. His father, Charles Phinney, is now over eighty years old ; his mother died of heart disease, at the age of 63 years ; her maiden name was Sarah Foster, and her parental home, Boston, Mass. Henry R. Phinney has been, since his majority, a wholesale dry grocer. At the present time, 1891, he is a stockholder, director, treasurer, and general manager of the Alton Improvement Association : — an Association owning real estate and the two City Railways, one propelled by motor power and the other by horses. The children of Lucretia Isham (Allen) and Henry R. Phinney, were :—

1 Mary Allen, born March 2, 1869, in Natchez, Miss.
2 Harriet Nye, born November 2, 1870, in Natchez, Miss.
3 Charles, born February 10, 1873, at Alton, Ill. ; died on Monday, February 23, 1878, at 6 A. M.
4 Lula Allen, born February 8, 1875, at Alton, Ill.
5 Henry R., born October 9, 1883, at Alton, Ill.

Mary Allen Phinney and Harriet Nye Phinney, were baptized in St. Paul's Church, Alton, by the Dean and Rector the Rev. Francis M. S. Taylor, in 1885. They were confirmed by the Right Rev. George Franklyn Seymour, S. T. D., LL. D., in St. Paul's, Alton, Ill., in 1887. Lula Allen was baptized by the Rev. Dr. Chase, and Henry R. Phinney, Jr., was baptized in 1885, by the Rev. F. M. S. Taylor.

Thomas Cushing Allen, fourth son and sixth child of Lewis Denison and Lucretia (Isham) Allen, was born April 16, 1848, in New London, Conn., and was baptized by the Rector, the Rev. Robert A. Hallam, D. D., in St. James' Church, in his infancy. He was a civil engineer on the Central and Southern Pacific Railroad for nine years and resigned to enter into mercantile business in Los Angelos, Cal., about two years ago, or in 1888.

Ansel Cady Allen, fifth son of Lewis Denison and Lucretia (Isham) Allen, was born May 11, 1850, in New London, Conn. He was baptized by the Rev. Robert A. Hallam, D. D., in St. James' Church, in his infancy. At the close of the War of the Rebellion, he was for about six years Deputy Post-master, at Natchez, Miss., and has been connected with Western Railroads in St. Louis, Miss., for many years, where he is highly esteemed for his efficiency ; he is associated at present with the St. Louis Freight Committee, at St. Louis, Miss. He is a prominent member of several secret Orders, and is a Past Noble Grand of Odd Fellows, and a Past Chancellor of Red Cross Lodge, No. 54, Knights of Pythias, of St. Louis.

Mary Smith, eldest daughter of Lewis and Mary Denison (Smith) Allen, was born on Fisher's Island, New York, July 8, 1808; she was baptized in infancy. She was married, May 9, 1832, to Enoch Vine Stoddard, at her father's residence. The ceremony was performed by the Rev. Bethel Judd, Rector of St. James' Church, New London, Conn. Enoch Vine Stoddard, who was born September 14, 1804, was the son of Vine and Prudence (Morgan) Stoddard. Vine Stoddard married, January 11, 1801, Sabria, daughter of Thomas and Hannah (Smith) Avery, who died August 7, 1803, and he married for his second wife Prudence (Morgan), widow of Gilbert Smith, second, to whom she had been married June 12, 1788, and by whom she had two sons, Erastus Tenant and Gilbert Avery Smith. Prudence (Morgan-Smith) was born April 16, 1768 : she was married to Vine Stoddard, November 23, 1803, and died in New London, April 9, 1865, aged 97 years. Vine Stoddard was born in Groton, Conn., October 28, 1775, and died December 27, 1863.

Enoch Vine, son of Vine and Prudence Stoddard, was a druggist in New London. He was Warden of St. James' Church for fifteen years. He died February 3, 1873, aged 69 years, 4 months and 20 days. His wife, Mary Smith (Allen) Stoddard, died January 5th, 1848, aged 39 years, 6 months and

2 days. She was beloved by all who knew her, a true Christian and a loving wife and mother. Husband and wife were buried in their lot, in the Cedar Grove Cemetery, New London. The children of Mary Smith (Allen) and Enoch Vine Stoddard were:

1 Mary Prudence, born March 17, 1838; was married June 27, 1861, and died February 6, 1871. [See below.]
2 Enoch Vine, Jr., born July 10, 1840; married June 3, 1868, and a second time, September 18, 1878. [See below.]
3 George, born January 16, 1843; married September 18, 1867. [See below.]
4 Harriet, born February 7, 1847; died July 23, 1853.

Mary Prudence, eldest daughter of Enoch Vine and Mary Smith (Allen) Stoddard, was born in New London, Conn., March 17, 1838; she was baptized in St. James' Church, by the Rev. Robert A. Hallam, D. D., and confirmed by the Right Rev. John Williams. She was married in St. James' Church, New London, Conn., at noon, June 27, 1861, by the Rector, the Rev. Dr. Hallam, to the Rev. Morelle Fowler. On their marriage certificate is the reference: Hebrews xiii, 20th and 21st verses, written by the Rev. Dr. Hallam. The Rev. Morelle Fowler, son of Victor and Sophia Fowler, was born at North Guilford, Conn., November 26, 1835. He was an assistant to the Rev. R. A. Hallam, D. D., in St. James' Church, New London, but left, the year of his marriage, to become the Rector of St. Paul's, Owego, N. Y. He was called from there to the Rectorship of St. James', Batavia, in the diocese of Western New York. From 1863 to 1868 he was a faithful pastor, and an earnest and eloquent preacher. His health failed, and he resigned his parish. He left New York City about 8 o'clock in the evening of February 6, on his way to Utah as a missionary, with his wife and three lovely children. At New Hamburg the Pacific Express, by which he was travelling, ran into an oil train, which was on fire, and itself caught fire. The bridge gave way, and the train went down with a crash. Mr. Fowler, with his wife and children, were all killed, and many others. It was said not one escaped that was in the sleeping-car with his party. Mrs. Fowler was found with two of her children clasped in her arms. The Rev. Mr. Fowler preached his farewell sermon, and assisted at the celebration of the Holy Communion, in St. Chrysostom's Chapel, in New York, on Sunday, the day before he started.

The following lines, by Eloise H. Thatcher, were suggested by the touching and impressive service at the funeral of Mr. Fowler and his family, in St James' Church, New London, Conn., Friday, February 10, 1871:

Three little coffins, flower-wreathed,
   Within God's holy temple stand;
Three little souls have gone to rest
Upon a loving Saviour's breast,
   Safely within the promised land.
A space between each little form
   Their parents' lifeless forms must fill;
They perished in one common fate,
   The ordering of God's righteous will!

Two coffined forms far down the aisle,
   Flower-strewn, and draped with sable pall,
Await the appointed messengers,
   Who bear the blessed Saviour's call.
One was a faithful priest of God,
   And zealous in his Master's Name;
The other, loving, and beloved
   As daughter, sister, mother, wife:
Both have " the fiery trial trod,"
   And perished amid frost and flame!
And both, we trust, their faith have proved,
   And won the crown of endless life.

A few brief years have passed away
   Since they before this altar came,
And in the bloom of early youth,
Plighted their vows of love and truth,
   Sealed by the blest Redeemer's Name.

The manly bridegroom, gentle bride,
  The Church her holiest blessing gave —
  Her love and care this side the grave.

And now upon the solemn scene
  A train of white-robed priests appear,
With saddened hearts and mournful mien,
  They bend beside each little bier :
And with a noiseless, reverent tread
Move down the aisle where wait the dead.
The Church to God now yields her trust,
With "earth to earth, and dust to dust."

" I am the resurrection and the life !"
  These cheering words fell on each sorrowing ear
As brother priests, in snowy vestments robed,
  Sadly along the aisle bear up the bier,
And loving brothers take the gentler form —
  They only should the sacred burden bear.
And now the vacant places, both are filled,
  And a whole family are gathered there.

None gone before ! God took them home together !
  Not disunited ! Not one left to weep !
Husband and wife can never more be parted !
  Parents and children in one grave shall sleep !
No little ones left, orphaned and alone —
  No widowed heart, bereft and desolate —
No rending of the heart-strings at the thought
  And memory of that sudden, fearful fate.
God in His wisdom hath ordained it so !
  God, in His love and mercy, took them all !
Above the gloom He bent His brightening bow,
  And lined with silver Death's dark, cloudy pall.

Their children, who perished with their parents, as already
stated, were :

1 Robert Hallam, born January 23, 1864, at St. James' Rectory,
    Batavia, N. Y.; baptized in St. James' Church, by the Rev.
    Orlando Witherspoon.
2 Agnes Stoddard, born January 13, 1866, in St. James' Rectory,
    Batavia, N. Y.; baptized by the Right Rev. Arthur Cleve-
    land Coxe, D. D., LL. D., in St. James' Church.

3 Morelle Worthington, born October 15, 1869, at North Guilford, Conn.; baptized by the Rev. Robert A. Hallam, D. D., in St. James' Church, in New London, Conn.

Enoch Vine Stoddard, Jr., eldest son of Enoch Vine and Mary Smith (Allen) Stoddard, was born in New London, Conn., July 10, 1840; he was baptized by the Rev. Robert A. Hallam, D. D., Rector of St. James' Church. He was graduated at Trinity College, Hartford, Conn., June, 1860, with the degree of B. A. He received the degree of A. M. in 1863 in course from his Alma Mater, and that of M. D. from the Albany Medical College, May 29, 1863. He entered the United States service at that date, and was in the army till near the close of the war. He married, June 3, 1868, Kate A. Conkey, in St. Luke's Church, Rochester, N. Y., the Rev. Morelle Fowler and the Rev. Henry Anstice, D. D., officiating. Kate A. Conkey was born June 11, 1845; she died September 5, 1869. They had no children. He married, as his second wife, September 18, 1878, Caroline Sarah Butts, who was born at Rochester, N. Y., September 18, 1850. The ceremony was performed at Rochester, N. Y., by his half brother, the Rev. James Stoddard, Rector of Christ Church, Watertown, Conn. They had two children:

1 Caroline Butts, born September 2, 1880, in Rochester, N. Y.
2 Enoch Vine, 3d, born June 20, 1883, in Rochester, N. Y. Both children were baptized by the Rev. Henry Anstice, Rector of St. Luke's, Rochester.

George Stoddard, second son of Enoch Vine and Mary Smith (Allen) Stoddard, was born in New London, Conn., January 16, 1843, and was baptized by the Rev. Robert A. Hallam, D. D., in St. James' Church. He went when young to Cincinnati, Ohio. He married, the Rev. John B. Wakefield officiating, in Cambridge City, Ind., September 18, 1867, Ida Louella Vinton. She was born March 22, 1849. The children of George and Ida Louella (Vinton) Stoddard were:

SARAH.   JANE.   ELIZABETH.   ELEANOR.   HARRIET.

DAUGHTERS OF LEWIS ALLEN   From Daguerreotype taken in 1849, at New London, Conn.

1 Thomas Vinton, born April 5, 1870, at Cambridge City, Ind.; baptized by the Rev. John B. Wakefield; died January 10, 1875.

2 Frederick Enoch, born September 25, 1871; baptized by the Rev. James Stoddard (brother of George Stoddard).

3 George Vinton, born December 21, 1873; baptized by the Rev. James Stoddard.

4 James Henry, born September 29, 1875; baptized in St. James' Church, New London, Conn., by the Rev. James Stoddard.

Frances Elizabeth, second daughter of Lewis and Mary Denison (Smith) Allen, was born on Fisher's Island, January 21, 1811; she was married at her father's, in New London, Conn., May 9, 1832, to Albigence Waldo Tucker, by the Rev. Bethel Judd, at that time Rector of St. James' Church. Mr. Tucker was a merchant in Walworth, N. Y., where they went to reside. He was born at Palmyra, N. Y., July 10, 1804; he died in New London, Conn., November 9, 1854, aged 50 years, 3 months, and 30 days. His widow died January 5, 1887, aged 75 years, 11 months, and 16 days, at her daughter's (Mrs. Henry Clay Brubaker), Lancaster, Penn. The children of Frances Elizabeth (Allen) and Albigence Waldo Tucker, were:

1 Lewis Albigence, born December 18, 1833, at Walworth, N. Y.; he was baptized in Palmyra, N. Y., by the Rev. Clement Butler, in his infancy. He was a private in the 9th Regiment, New York Volunteers, and died at Key West, Fla., June, 1862.

2 George Allen, born June 3, 1836, at Walworth, N. Y.; baptized in Palmyra, N. Y.; died February 25, 1840.

3 Edward Augustus, born June 27, 1840, at Walworth, N. Y.; baptized by the Rev. Clement Butler, in Zion Church, Palmyra, N. Y.; died January 2, 1841.

4 Edward Augustus (second of the name), born January 3, 1842, at New London, Conn.; baptized in St. James' Church, by the Rev. Robert A. Hallam, D. D.; died June 25, 1876.

5 Isabel, born July 26, 1846, at New London, Conn.; baptized
   in St. James' Church, by the Rev. Robert A. Hallam, D. D.;
   she was married April 23, 1867. [See below.]
6 Jane Allen, born November 6, 1848, at New London, Conn.;
   baptized by the Rev. R. A. Hallam, D. D.
7 Mary Elizabeth, born March 14, 1851, at New London, Conn.;
   baptized by the Rev. R. A. Hallam, D. D., in St. James'
   Church; she was married April 29, 1869.

Isabel Tucker, eldest daughter of Albigence Waldo and
Frances Elizabeth (Allen) Tucker, was born at New London,
Conn., July 26, 1846. She was confirmed by the Right Rev.
Arthur Cleveland Coxe, D. D., LL.D.; she was married at
Trinity Church, Buffalo, N. Y., April 23, 1867, to John Smith
Shackelford, by the Rev. Edward Ingersol, Rector of that
parish. Mr. Shackelford was born in Lynchburg, Va., August
28, 1833. He died in Columbus, O., January 17, 1877, aged
43 years, 4 months, and 20 days. They had three children :

1 Bella Strader, born February 4, 1868, at Indianapolis, Ind.;
   she was baptized by the Rev. J. P. T. Ingraham, in that
   city.
2 William Ernest, born February 19, 1871, at Columbus, O.; he
   was baptized by the Rev. Rufus W. Clark, D. D., in Columbus, O.
3 Blanche, born June 29, 1873, at Columbus, O.; she was baptized by the Rev. Rufus W. Clark, D. D., in the same place.

Mary Elizabeth, youngest daughter of Albigence Waldo
and Frances Elizabeth (Allen) Tucker, was born at New London, Conn., March 14, 1841; she was confirmed by the Right
Rev. George Upfold, S.T.D., LL.D., first Bishop of Indiana;
she was married in Cambridge, Ind., Thursday, April 29, 1869,
by the Rev. John B. Wakefield, Rector of St. Paul's Church,
Richmond, Ind., to Henry Clay Brubaker, who was born at
Lancaster, Penn., March 5, 1843. He is an attorney-at-law,
and was elected District Judge in May, 1891. The children
of Mary Elizabeth (Tucker) and Henry Clay Brubaker are :

1 Ellen Allen, born February 22, 1870, at Lancaster, Penn.; she
   was baptized by the Rev. Dr. Walton, Rector of St. James'
   Church, Lancaster.

2 George Stuart Wylie, born March 8, 1872, at Lancaster, Penn.;
   he was baptized in St. James' Church by the Rector, Rev.
   Dr. Watson.

3 Henry Clay, born May 3, 1874, at Lancaster, Penn.; he was
   baptized by the Rev. Dr. Watson.

4 Mary Tucker, born February 6, 1876, at Lancaster, Penn.; she
   was baptized by the Rev. Dr. Watson.

5 Elizabeth Allen, born December 15, 1877, at Lancaster, Penn.;
   she was baptized by the Rev. Cyrus Frederic Knight, then
   Rector of St. James' Church (afterwards Bishop of Mil-
   waukee).

6 Waldo Tucker, born March 10, 1880, at Lancaster, Penn.; he
   was baptized in St. James' Church, by the Rector, the Rev.
   Cyrus F. Knight, D. D.

7 James Frederick, born April 2, 1882, at Lancaster, Penn.; he
   was baptized in St. James' Church, by the Rector, the Rev.
   Dr. Knight.

8 William Mercer, born August 2, 1884, at Lancaster, Penn.; he
   was baptized by the Rev. Dr. Knight.

9 Lewis Allen, born December 10, 1890, at Lancaster, Penn.: he
   was baptized at St. James' Church, March 14, 1891, by the
   Rector, the Rev. P. J. Robottom. His sponsors were Lewis
   Denison Allen (great-uncle of the child, and for whom he
   was named), Henry Clay Brubaker, Jr., and Mrs. Ellie P.
   Spurrie.

Harriet Amelia, third daughter of Lewis and Mary Denison
(Smith) Allen, was born at Pequonnoc, Conn., September 25,
1813; she was baptized, in September, 1816, by the Rev.
Solomon Blakesley, who was then the Rector of St. James'
Church, New London, Conn. She was married, at her
father's, on the evening of December 21, 1841, to Ansel C.
Cady, by the Rev. Robert A. Hallam, D. D., then Rector of
St. James' Church. Mr. Cady was a merchant in New Lon-
don, Conn., and died in that city, November 26, 1845. The

children of Harriet Amelia (Allen) and Ansel C. Cady were born at New London, and were as follows :

1 Frederick Lee Allen, born April 24, 1843; married June 7, 1870. [See below.]
2 Ansel C. Cady, Jr., born June 10, 1845 ; died March 23, 1848.

Mrs. Cady, after the death of her husband, went to Buffalo, N. Y., to reside. She was married, December 20, 1852, to her second husband, Thomas Goodman Perkins. He was a widower, with one daughter, Ellen, who married Frederick B. Squires. He died December 1, 1880. The children of Thomas G. and Harriet Amelia (Allen-Cady) Perkins were :

1 Thomas Goodman, born May 23, 1856 ; married April 20, 1882. [See below.]
2 George Hazzard, born June 10, 1859.

Frederick Lee Allen Cady, eldest son of Ansel C. and Harriet Amelia (Allen) Cady, was born at New London, Conn., April 24, 1843 ; he was baptized by the Rev. Dr. Hallam, in St. James' Church, and was confirmed by the Right Rev. Arthur Cleveland Coxe, D. D., LL. D., Bishop of Western New York, in Trinity Church, Buffalo, N. Y. He is in the insurance business ; the firm has been Stringer & Cady for twenty-five years. Frederick Lee Allen Cady and Jeanie Stimson were married June 7, 1870, by the Rev. John M. Henderson, assisted by the Rev. Edward Ingersoll, D. D., in the Church of the Ascension, at Buffalo, N. Y. Jeanie Stimson Cady was the daughter of M. R. and Helen Warren Stimson, and was born January 6, 1848 ; she was confirmed in Trinity Church, Buffalo, N. Y., by the Right Rev. Bishop Coxe. Clarence White, the only child of Frederick Lee Allen and Jeanie (Stimson) Cady was born at Buffalo, N. Y., September 9, 1871 ; he was baptized by the Rev. Edward Ingersoll, D. D., February 2, 1872. He entered Harvard College in September, 1889.

Thomas Goodman Perkins, Jr., eldest son of Thomas Goodman and Harriet Amelia (Allen) Perkins, was born at Buffalo, N. Y., May 23, 1856; he was baptized by the Rector, the Rev. Edward Ingersoll, D. D., in Trinity Church, Buffalo, and was confirmed in the same Church by the Right Rev. Bishop Coxe. He is in the insurance business in Buffalo, N. Y. He married Lizzie Blair Atwater, at Buffalo, N. Y., April 20, 1882, the Rev. William Shelton, D. D., and the Rev. Edward Ingersoll, D. D., Rectors of St. Paul's and Trinity Churches, officiating. Lizzie Blair Atwater was the daughter of Edward M. and Maria Smith Atwater, and was born October 15, 1861 ; she was confirmed by Bishop Coxe, at St. Paul's Church, Buffalo, N. Y. Their children, who were born at Buffalo, are :

1 Marion, born August 29, 1883.
2 Allen Seymour, born July 4, 1885.
3 Mildred, born September 29, 1887. Marion, Allen Seymour, and Mildred were all baptized by the Rector, the Rev. John W. Brown, D. D., in St. Paul's Church, Buffalo, N. Y.

George Hazzard, younger son of Thomas Goodman and Harriet Amelia (Allen) Perkins, was born at Buffalo, N. Y., June 10, 1859 ; he was baptized by the Rev. Edward Ingersoll, D. D., in Trinity Church, in that city, and was confirmed by Bishop Coxe in the same Church. He married, in 1890, Adele Madeline Bleiler, who was born in 1869.

Sarah Ann, fourth daughter of Lewis and Mary Denison (Smith) Allen [see page 51] was born at Pequonnoc, Conn., May 4, 1817. She was baptized by the Rev. Solomon Blakesley, in St. James' Church, New London, Conn., and was confirmed by the Right Rev. Thomas Church Brownell, D. D., Bishop of Connecticut, in the same Church. She was married, as his second wife, to Enoch Vine Stoddard, January 15th, 1849, in New London, the Rev. Robert A. Hallam, D. D., officiating. Enoch Vine Stoddard was born

September 14, 1804, and died February 3, 1874,* aged 69 years, 4 months, and 20 days. The children of Enoch Vine and Sarah Ann (Allen) Stoddard were:

1 James, born December 20, 1849. [See below.]
2 Henry Haven, born March 22, 1854; he was baptized by the Rev. Dr. Hallam, in St. James' Church. [See below.]
3 Sarah Allen, born February 22, 1856; she was baptized by the Rev. Dr. Hallam, in St. James' Church.
4 Charlotte Morgan, born March 2, 1858; she was baptized by the Rev. Dr. Hallam. [See below.]

Enoch Vine Stoddard, whose parentage has been given on a previous page, went to New London in 1820, and became a clerk for Dr. Isaac Thompson, a leading druggist. He conducted the drug business (for he became a partner) until 1845, when he retired, and formed a co-partnership with Edward H. Learned, under the firm of Stoddard & Learned, for the prosecution of the whale fishery. More than seventy whaling vessels were enrolled from that port. He received the rite of confirmation, and became a communicant of St. James' Church, in 1840. After that time he was Vestryman or Warden while he lived.

James, eldest son of Enoch Vine and Sarah Ann (Allen) Stoddard, was born in New London, Conn., December 20, 1849. He was baptized June 11, 1850, by the Rev. Robert A. Hallam, D. D., in the new St. James' Church, the first to be baptized in it, immediately after its consecration; he was confirmed by the Right Rev. John Williams, S. T. D., LL. D., Bishop of Connecticut, April 26, 1863. He graduated at Trinity College, Hartford, June 28, 1871. He studied Theology at the Berkeley Divinity School, Middletown, Conn., and was ordained to the Diaconate by Bishop Williams, in the Church of the Holy Trinity, Middletown, May 28, 1874. He was ordained Priest in St. James' Church, New London, on St. Barnabas' Day, June 11, 1875, by Bishop Williams, and

---

* On p. 58 (*supra*) the year is erroneously given in 1873.

became the Rector of St. James' Church, Westville, Conn., October 15, 1875; of Christ Church, at Watertown, Conn., January 1, 1877, and of St. Mark's, New Britain, Conn., April 1, 1886. He married, in New York City, April 27, 1881, Alice Kent, daughter of George Lewis and Matilda Jane (Rockwell) Kent, Bishop Williams of Connecticut performing the ceremony. The children of James and Alice (Kent) Stoddard are :

1 Virginia Toyan, born February 14, 1882, at Watertown, Conn.; she was baptized by Bishop Williams, in Christ Church, May 28, 1882.

2 Alice Kent, born August 29, 1883, at Watertown, Conn.; she was baptized October 24, 1883.

3 Sarah Allen, born June 5, 1885, at Watertown, Conn.; she was baptized January 6, 1886.

4 George Kent, born January 13, 1888, at New Britain, Conn.; he was baptized March 24, 1888.

5 James Kent, born Monday morning, January 26, 1891, at New Britain; he was baptized April 26, 1891.

Henry Haven, second son of Enoch Vine and Sarah Ann (Allen) Stoddard, was born at New London, Conn., March 22, 1854. He was baptized by the Rev. Dr. Hallam, in St. James' Church, New London, Conn., and was confirmed, May 28, 1890, by the Right Rev. Bishop Williams, in the same Church, the Rev. J. F. Bingham, D. D., then being the Rector. He married, at Zion Church, New York City, April 22, 1884, Marie Day McEwen, his brother, the Rev. James Stoddard, assisted by the Rev. Charles C. Tiffany, D. D., Rector of Zion Church, officiating. Marie Day McEwen, daughter of Dr. John B. and Mary (Day) McEwen, was born December 31, 1858; she was baptized at her father's house in New York City, when she was two years old, by the Rev. Henry Montgomery, D. D. The water used for the sacrament was brought from the river Jordan, in Syria, by the Rev. Dr. Montgomery. She was confirmed, May 25, 1876, by the Right Rev. Horatio Potter, Bishop of New York, in the Church of the Incarnation, of which the Rev. Arthur Brooks is Rector. Henry Haven Stoddard is a manufacturer.

The only child of Henry Haven and Marie Day (McEwen) Stoddard is named Marie Day ; she was born in New London, Conn., October 14, 1885, in the same room of the same house where her father was born, and where he had always lived. She was baptized by her uncle, the Rev. James Stoddard, February 12, 1886, in St. James' Church, New London.

Charlotte Morgan, daughter and youngest child of Enoch Vine and Sarah Ann (Allen) Stoddard, was born at New London, Conn., March 2, 1858, and was baptized in St. James' Church, by the Rev. Dr. Hallam. She was confirmed by Bishop Williams of Connecticut, in the same Church, and was married in that Church, October 7, 1884, by her brother, the Rev. James Stoddard, assisted by the Rev. Theodore Babcock, D. D., (father of the groom) and the Rev. William B. Buckingham, to Henry Nash Babcock, second son of the Rev. Theodore and Elizabeth (Nash) Babcock. He was born at Ballston Spa, N. Y., and baptized in the same place. He was confirmed in Trinity Church, Watertown, N. Y., in 1865, by the Right Rev. Arthur Cleveland Coxe, then Assistant Bishop of Western New York. Mr. Babcock was graduated at Rensselaer Polytechnic Institute, Troy, N. Y., in 1870. The children of Charlotte Morgan (Stoddard) and Henry Nash Babcock were :

1 Sarah, born September 27, 1886, at New London, Conn. ; she was baptized by the Rev. James Stoddard, in St. James' Church, December 27, 1886 ; she died at Yonkers, N. Y., March 18, 1887.

2 Theodore Stoddard, born February 26, 1888, at "Pelham Manor," Pelham, Long Island, N. Y.; he was baptized at Christ Church, Pelham, April 15, 1888, by the Rev. Theodore Babcock, D. D.

3 Henry Stoddard, born December 15, 1890, at Pelham, N. Y.; he was baptized at home, by his uncle, the Rev. James Stoddard, Rector of Christ Church, New Britain, Conn., April 10, 1891.

LEWIS ALLEN.

ENOCH VINE STODDARD.

FREDERICK L. ALLEN.

FREDERICK L. ALLEN Jr.

Frederick Lee Allen, second son and sixth child of Lewis and Mary Denison (Smith) Allen, was born at New London, Conn., May 20, 1820; he was baptized by the Rev. Bethel Judd, D. D., Rector, in St. James' Church. He married Wait Harris Lippett, June 4, 1849, in Westerly, R. I., the Rev. Thomas Hubbard Vail, afterwards Bishop of Kansas, officiating. Wait Harris (Lippett) Allen was born May 5, 1823; she was confirmed by the Right Rev. Thomas March Clark, D. D., LL. D., in Christ Church, Westerly, R. I. Mr. Allen was a druggist; for six years he was Mayor of New London; in 1866 he was elected for three years, and in 1869 was re-elected for another term of three years. In that position he proved himself a capable, independent, incorruptible and devoted servant of the public interests. In 1867 he was elected Representative for New London in the General Assembly, and again in 1868. In 1871 he was elected State Senator from the Seventh District, by a large majority, running far ahead of his associates on the Democratic ticket, and for many years he was recognized as one of the leaders of that party in the State, and his local popularity was almost unbounded. He never stooped to dishonorable practices; he was strong with the people, because they believed him honest in his convictions and frank and fearless in his actions. It has been said that there was no office in the gift of his party, in that State, which would not have been willingly bestowed upon him. Mr. Allen died February 27, 1872, aged 51 years, 9 months, and 7 days. His disease was pneumonia; he was sick but a few days. "The loss of Mr. Allen in the maturity of his life was keenly felt in the community. His last act, before leaving his place of business, was like him, and put a beautiful cap-stone on his character. A colored man begging, a wretched looking wayfarer seeking alms, went into his store, and presented letters of recommendation. Mr. Allen never read the letters, but dropped them indifferently upon the show-case, looked in the face of the woe-begone stroller, gave him a sum of money, took his hat, and went home to die.

The hand of death was on him, but it found him with his heart full of the same old charities, and his hand acting unitedly with his heart. The Hon. Frederick L. Allen was a noble and generous man, and dearly loved by his family and all who knew him." I append to this a tribute from a New London newspaper, printed the day after his funeral, which took place from St. James' Church:

Yesterday was the saddest day New London ever saw. Everybody stood under the shadow and felt the presence of a peculiar and absorbing sorrow. On no such occasion was the exhibition of genuine grief ever so marked in this town, or so unrestrained and unanimous. There was one common consent about closing the stores; the tribute was not even suggested, yet not the smallest place or most obscure shop in the whole town was open. Everyone had lost a friend, and each took the most natural and decided way to express his sorrow. Every flag was at half-mast. The fishing fleet, to whom he had been such a friend both in his public and private character, lowered their colors and remained at the wharves out of respect to his memory. No business was done. . . Was ever a public expression of affliction manifested so unanimously, without any common understanding as to method or uniformity?

The beautiful tribute was spontaneous and irrespective of all classification. It was therefore appropriate, for all classes claimed him. Such an ovation of sorrow was never seen before. When the great simooms sweep over the deserts, all life, by a common instinct, kneels down until the horror has passed over. So when a great death calamity like the present one visits a community, then from an irresistible instinct of respect, the people all kneel down and acknowledge with united voice the impartial affliction. The dust of this desert of sorrow here yesterday covered over the mortal remains of Frederic L. Allen.

Somehow we have never associated Death with him or his name. He seemed too strong, too useful, too kingly-noble to die. His great strength, his unconquerable vitality, his sterling spirit, all appeared to be too mighty for the grim destroyer; and yet he is dead, and died like a child without a murmur and with his heart as warm and his frame as firm as ever. We believe the great golden gates of the beautiful land were rolled far back when this regal soul went in. It had done its work here—some great but congenial task of love and generosity lies now before it.

The funeral took place yesterday afternoon at St. James' Episcopal Church, of which the deceased was a Vestryman. The Church was crowded long before the time announced for the services to begin, and amidst the mournful peals of the organ, while the vast congregation sat in silence and tears, the body of the beloved departed, laid in a rosewood casket upon which were placed a floral cross and crown, was brought in. Then followed the reading of that chapter of Scripture written by St. Paul, which overflows with religious rapture, and wherein the Apostle, in sanctified exultation, exclaims, "O Death, where is thy sting? O Grave, where is thy victory?"

The services were conducted by the Rev. Dr. Hallam and the Rev. Mr. Hutchings, upon the conclusion of which the remains were uncovered to the view of the vast throng of mourners, every one of whom was visibly affected. Between two and three thousand people were in the street, tearfully anxious for a parting look at the face of him they loved. For almost an hour they marched by him, their faces looking alike with the impress of grief upon them. Nameaug Engine Company acted as an escort, in compliance with his cherished wish. He was the founder and father of the company, and he loved and encouraged it to the day of his earthly end.

The very Church seemed to be suggestive of the dead, and to bring his figure in life, and not his form in death before us. Every rare and exquisite color of glass, reflected and repeated in a rarer and still more exquisite ray, seemed to symbol some rare and delicate act of his life, oft repeated with still finer tenderness!

Bereavement acts upon the emotional organization like amputation upon the body. For a time we are benumbed and quiet, then follows agony, and finally the severed limb seems to be restored again, and all our feelings and sensations appear to centre there. So with this bereavement; at first we were stunned and passive, then came acute and uncontrollable grief, and now we almost feel as if he were still alive and with us!

On the first day of Spring we buried him. On the opening of that time when the flowers come up and all the birds make music in the air, how blessed it is to believe that when that Spring of resurrection comes, when the souls of men spring forth like the flowers, we shall see him again.

Come soon, robin, with your breast of sacred red, and bluebird with the tint of Heaven under your wing, come and sing at his grave.

His brother, Thomas H. C. Allen, of Cincinnati, O., has erected a granite monument at his grave. One of the local newspapers, in speaking of it, said:

To the memory of a great heart, and to the memory of a man who thought of others first and himself last, to the memory of Frederick L. Allen, a granite monument is now placed in position upon his grave in beautiful Cedar Grove Cemetery. Every man, woman and child in New London who reads this mournful but gratifying announcement will feel a thrill of pleasurable gratitude therefor. If all the benevolent deeds he did every day of his stirring life — if all the secret charities from his hands were to take upon themselves the ostentation of granite, lofty would be the shaft that towered over his flowering grave.

So beneath this brotherly tribute will sleep on "great-hearted Fred," until the angel of immortality shall roll away from the universal grave of man all stones and slabs and monuments; and we, who have only taken on the mortal form of life here, will assume it in imperishable fact there.

The children of Frederick Lee and Wait Harris (Lippett) Allen were:

1 Frederick Lee, Jr., born July 20, 1851, at Westerly, R. I. [See below.]
2 Mary, born March 31, 1855, at New London; died April 2, 1855.
3 Florence Lippett, born January 8, 1858, at New London. [See below.]
4 Sebastian Lawrence, born February 21, 1860, at New London; died November 14, 1861.

Frederick Lee Allen, Jr., was born in Westerly, R. I., July 20, 1851. He was baptized in St. James' Church, by the Rev. Dr. Hallam, and confirmed the second Sunday after

Thomas H. C. Allen

Trinity, April 27, 1873, by the Right Rev. Bishop Williams. He married, in New London, May 8, 1877, Mary Ida Dow, the Rev. William B. Buckingham, Rector of St. James' Church, officiating. Mary Ida (Dow) Allen was born in August, 1853; she was the daughter of Isaac Wilson and Mary Elizabeth Dow. She died from dropsy, August 7, 1883, at nine, P. M.; the funeral service was held at her late residence, and the burial from St. James' Church. The children of Frederick Lee and Mary Ida (Dow) Allen were:

1 Frederick Lee (3d), born October 3, 1878, at New London, Conn.; he was baptized, December 30, 1880, by the Rev. James Stoddard.
2 Wilson Frank, } twins, born August 1, 1883.
3 Elizabeth Wait, }
   Wilson Frank died August 29, 1883; Elizabeth Wait died September 3, 1883. They were baptized, August 23, 1883, by the Rev. William B. Buckingham.

Frederick Lee Allen, Jr., married, Tuesday, July 1, 1891, as his second wife, Martha Kate Denison, daughter of the late R. S. Denison, of New London, Conn., the Rev. Mr. Bixler officiating. They reside in Providence, R. I.

Florence Lippett Allen was baptized by the Rev. Dr. Hallam, and confirmed by Bishop Williams of Connecticut, November, 17, 1887, in St. James' Church, New London, Conn. She was married November 17, 1887, at the residence of her mother, Mrs. Frederick Lee Allen, by the Rev. A. Douglass Miller, Rector of St. James', to Frank S. Boyce, of Providence, R. I.

Thomas Humphrey Cushing Allen, third son and seventh child of Lewis and Mary Denison Allen, was born September 21, 1822, at New London, Conn.; he was baptized by the Rector, the Rev. Bethel Judd, in St. James' Church, New London; he was confirmed in 1853 by the Right Rev. Charles P. McIlvaine, Bishop of Ohio, at St. John's Church, Cincinnati, O., of which the Rev. William R. Nicholson, D. D., was then the Rector.

Mr. Allen married in Cincinnati, the Rev. Dr. Nicholson officiating, on June 1, 1852, Jane Deverdier Woodruff, daughter of Truman and Mary Woodruff. She was born September 1, 1832, in Hartford, Conn. ; she was an invalid for many years, and died August 30, 1878, aged 45 years, 11 months and 30 days. She was interred in the Allen lot, in Spring Grove Cemetery, Cincinnati, O. The children of Thomas H. C. and Jane Deverdier (Woodruff) Allen, who were born in Cincinnati, O., were :

1 William Mercer, born February 25, 1853. [See below.]
2 Thomas Woodruff, born September 26, 1855. [See below.]
3 Jonathan Harris, born June 17, 1859. [See below.]

Thomas H. C. Allen went in the spring of 1840, to reside in Salina, now the first Ward of Syracuse, N. Y., then the great salt-mart of the West, but returned to New London, Conn., his native place, in 1842 ; he was in business there until the spring of 1848, when he went to Cincinnati, O., and established the medicine business. After introducing " Perry Davis' Pain Killer " throughout the west and south-west, he brought out "Allen's Lung Balsam," and introduced that throughout the United States and Canada and into some foreign countries. He has continued to manage that business with success and profit to himself and all interested with him, and with relief to suffering humanity. Mr. Allen is a Director of both Life and Fire Insurance Companies, of Bank and Charitable Institutions, and President of the only Savings Bank in Cincinnati (1892).

He was Vestryman, or Warden, of St. John's Church, Cincinnati, for twenty-eight years, resigning in 1883. He assisted in forming the Church of Our Saviour, on Mount Auburn, Cincinnati, in 1876 ; he was chairman of the first meeting to organize the Parish, and its first Warden, and contributed liberally towards the erection of the lovely edifice, which has been enlarged twice, and is now (1892) one of the most beautiful and churchly buildings in Southern Ohio. Mr. Allen has

ERECTED IN 1853.　　　　HOME OF THOMAS H. C. ALLEN.　　　　MT. AUBURN, CINCINNATI, OHIO.

been its Senior Warden since resigning that position at St. John's, 1883, and has shown his deep interest in its success, not only pecuniarily, but in every way possible, and the Parish is out of debt, and self-sustaining. The Rev. Dudley Ward Rhodes is the only Rector which this Church has had, now (1892) serving his sixteenth year.

Mr. Allen moved to Mount Auburn, a suburb of Cincinnati, and built the house in which he now lives, in 1853, when his oldest son, William Mercer, was only four months old. In 1886, he built on lots adjoining the homestead, a block of three houses, with stone front, for his three sons,—William Mercer, Thomas Woodruff and Jonathan Harris Allen. They are all married and reside in them, and fully appreciate their father's valuable gift.

Mr. Allen married as his second wife, Laura Alice Rowe, (daughter of Stanhope and Frances M. Rowe,) August 5, 1879, the Rev. Dudley W. Rhodes, their Rector, officiating. Laura Alice Rowe was born July 7, 1853, in Cincinnati, O. They have two children :

1 Charlotte Rowe, born January 18, 1887, in Cincinnati, O.; she was baptized on Trinity Sunday, June 5, 1887, at the Church of Our Saviour, by the Rev. Dudley W. Rhodes.

2 Frederick Lewis, born at 4 P. M., Monday, February 2, 1891; he was baptized May 31, 1891, in the Church of Our Saviour, by the Rector, the Rev. Dudley W. Rhodes. His sponsors were :—William M. Allen, his uncle, Alfred I. Totten, from Lexington, Ky., and Marietta B. Handy. He and his nephew, Douglass Marshall Allen, [son of Jonathan H. Allen,] were baptized at the same time.

William Mercer, eldest son of Thomas Humphrey Cushing and Jane Deverdier (Woodruff) Allen, was born in Cincinnati, O., February 25, 1853; he was baptized in Connersville, Ind., by the Rev. Mr. Stuart; his sponsors were Lewis Denison Allen, Lucretia (Isham) Allen, and his parents. He married, at Cincinnati, O., October 5, 1876, Virginia Reakirt Thompson, daughter of Moses F. Thompson, the Rev. E. D. Ledyard officiating. She was born August 25, 1856, Their children are :

1 Florence Ferne, born July 29, 1877 ; she was baptized by the Rt. Rev. Thos. A. Jaggar, Bishop of Southern Ohio, at Fern Bank ; she was confirmed, April 7, 1891, by the Right Rev. Thomas Underwood Dudley, Bishop of Kentucky, in the Church of Our Saviour, Mount Auburn, Cincinnati.

2 Anna Louise, born March 22, 1880 ; baptized by the Rev. Charles M. Sturges, in the Church of the Resurrection at Fern Bank, Ohio.

3 Stanley Woodruff, born March 6, 1887 ; baptized October 9, 1887, after Morning Prayer, by the Rector, in the Church of Our Saviour, Mount Auburn, Cincinnati. His sponsors were his grandfathers, Moses F. Thompson and Thomas H. C. Allen, and his parents.

4 William Thompson Allen, born October 16, 1891.

William Mercer Allen is a Vestryman of the Church of Our Saviour, and the Superintendent of the Sunday School.

Thomas Woodruff Allen, second son of Thomas Humphrey Cushing and Jane Deverdier Allen, was born at Cincinnati, O., September 26, 1855 ; he was baptized in the Chapel at Connersville, Ind.; the sponsors were his uncle and aunt, Lewis Denison and Lucretia (Isham) Allen, and his father, Thomas H. C. Allen ; the sacrament was administered by the Rector, the Rev. Mr. Stuart. He married Emily Meigs Keith, on Wednesday evening, November 23, 1881, the Rev. A. H. Partridge officiating ; the wedding took place at 189 South Oxford Street, Brooklyn, N. Y. Mrs. Emily M. Allen was born May 19, 1857. After their marriage they went to San Jose, Costa Rica, Central America, for Mrs. Allen's health. Their only child, Thomas Minor Keith, was born in San Jose, Costa Rica, April 13, 1883, and was baptized by the Rev. Dudley W. Rhodes. Mr. Allen and his wife and child came North, and she died September 23, 1884. Thomas Woodruff

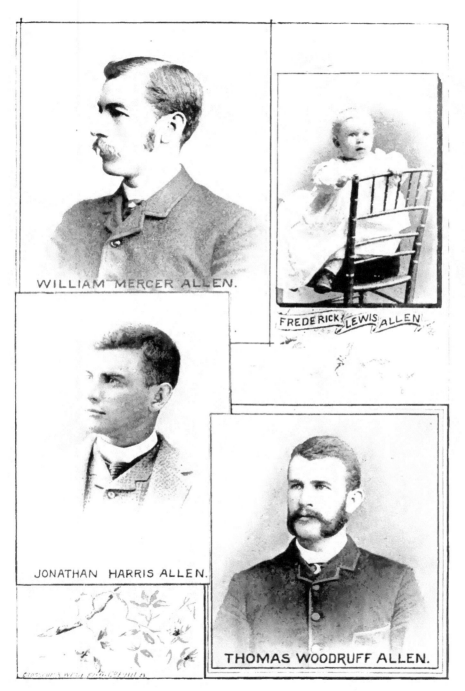

WILLIAM MERCER ALLEN.

FREDERICK LEWIS ALLEN

JONATHAN HARRIS ALLEN.

THOMAS WOODRUFF ALLEN.

SONS OF THOMAS H. C. ALLEN.

Allen married in New York City, October 6, 1885, Annie Huntington, as his second wife, the Rev. Theodore A. Eaton officiating. She was born February 19, 1858. They reside in Cincinnati, O. ; he is engaged in mercantile pursuits. The children of Thomas W. and Annie Allen are :

1 Raynor Huntington, born May 17, 1887, at Cincinnati, O. ; he was baptized by the Rev. Dudley W. Rhodes, in the Church of Our Saviour, October 9, 1887. His sponsors were Walter W. Conklin, Gertrude H. Conklin, and his father, Thomas W. Allen.

2 Grace de Silver, born July 15, 1889, at Cincinnati, O. ; she was baptized in the Church of Our Saviour, Easter Even, April 5, 1890, by the Rev. Dudley W. Rhodes, her parents being her sponsors.

3 Walter Woodruff, born August 17, 1891, at Cincinnati, O.

Jonathan Harris Allen, third son of Thomas Humphrey Cushing and Jane Deverdier Allen, was born at Cincinnati, O., June 17, 1859; he was baptized in his infancy. He married on Wednesday, December 1, 1886, in the Church of Our Saviour, Mount Auburn, Cincinnati, Anna Williamson Handy. A Cincinnati paper has the following account :

ALLEN—HANDY.

A very pretty wedding was celebrated yesterday afternoon at the Church of Our Saviour. The bride was Miss Anna Williamson Handy, youngest daughter of the late Truman B. Handy, and the groom Mr. Jona. Harris Allen, son of Mr. T. H. C. Allen, of Mt. Auburn. The ceremony took place at five o'clock, the Rector of the Parish, the Rev. Dudley W. Rhodes, brother-in-law of the bride, officiating. The beautiful Church was gaily decorated with chrysanthemums and crowded to the doors with friends of the happy pair.

The bride wore a charming toilet of white silk and lace and carried a bouquet of Niphetos rosebuds and lilies of the valley. Her maids were Miss Helen Louise Thoms, maid of honor; Miss Alice Ferguson and Miss Mattie Hanna, who were dressed quite alike in frocks of white mousseline de Saxe, with V-shaped bodices

of white moiré. The bride was met at the altar by the groom,
accompanied by his best man, Mr. Harry W. Leonard, of Chicago,
and was given in marriage by her brother, Mr. Charles E. Handy,
of Minneapolis. Miss Hattie Doughty, organist of Calvary Church,
Clifton, presided at the organ and played with even more than her
accustomed grace and skill.

The ushers were Mr. Horace Taft, Mr. Nelson Strobridge, Mr.
Guy Mallon and Mr. Harry Talbot. After the ceremony a collation
was served to the immediate families of bride and groom, at the
home of the bride, McMillan Street, under the direction of Becker.
The gift of Mr. Allen, Sr., to his son, is an elegantly furnished
house, one of the block of artistic stone houses which he built last
summer, on Auburn Avenue. Here the happy pair will set up
their lares and penates on their return from their honeymoon, and
will be " at home " Fridays in January.

The children of Jonathan Harris and Anna Williamson
(Handy) Allen are:

1 Carrie Louise, born October 28, 1887, at Cincinnati, O.; bap-
   tized by the Rev. Dudley W. Rhodes, in the Church of Our
   Saviour, March 18, 1888. Her sponsors were Mrs. Jennie
   (Handy) Rhodes, Mrs. Carrie Collins, and her uncle,
   Thomas Woodruff Allen.

2 Thomas Humphrey Cushing, 2d, born May 22, 1889, at Cin-
   cinnati, O. He was baptized in the Church of Our Saviour,
   Easter Even, April 5, 1890, by the Rev. Dudley W. Rhodes.
   His sponsors were his grandfather, Thomas H. C. Allen
   (Senior Warden of that Parish), and his parents.

3 Douglass Marshall, born April 10, 1891, at Cincinnati, O.; he
   was baptized by the Rev. Dudley W. Rhodes, May 31, 1891,
   at the Church of Our Saviour, where they had a special
   Service at 4.30 P. M., because his uncle, Frederick Lewis
   Allen was baptized at the same time. Seldom are uncle
   and nephew carried to the font together, to have the same
   Service used for both. Douglas Marshall Allen's sponsors
   were his uncle, Thomas Woodruff Allen, Mrs. Howard
   Douglas, and his father, Jonathan Harris Allen.

Jane Cellina, fifth daughter and eighth child of Lewis and Mary Denison (Smith) Allen, was born in New London, Conn., June 28, 1824. She was baptized in her infancy, by the Rev. Bethel Judd, D. D., Rector of St. James' Church, New London, and confirmed by the Right Rev. Manton Eastburn, Bishop of Massachusetts, in St. Paul's Church, Boston. She was married to Worthington Buckley Button, May 8, 1848, by the Rev. Robert A. Hallam, D. D., Rector of St. James' Church, New London, Conn.

Worthington Buckley Button was born at Hampton, Conn., May 16, 1822 ; he was baptized in St. James' Church, New London, August 15, 1873, by the Rector, Rev. Dr. Hallam. Mr. Button was a merchant in Boston, Mass., and in New York, for many years. He was a genial and kind man, very hospitable, and much beloved by those who knew him. He was a son of Charles C. and Lucy (Thurston) Button. He died (of Bright's disease) in his native place, July 22, 1882, aged 60 years and 2 months. Mrs. Jane Cellina (Allen) Button died at the home of her daughter, Mrs. James C. Church, in Boston, May 8, 1890, aged 65 years, 10 months, and 10 days. Hers was a life of perfect usefulness, and loving deeds, and helpful words, for all with whom she had intercourse ; her crosses were heavy, her crown will be glorious. The children of Worthington Buckley and Jane Cellina (Allen) Button were :

1 Harriet Cady, born April 26, 1849, at New London, Conn. ; baptized in her infancy by the Rev. Dr. Hallam. She was married, February 2, 1881, to George Remington Burroughs, the Rev. Henry A. Coleman officiating. Mr. Burroughs was born November 27, 1838 ; he was a member of the Connecticut Legislature in 1888–1889. They have one child, Horace Worthington Burroughs, born December 27, 1882, at Hampton, Conn.

2 Lucy Thurston, born June 28, 1852, at New London, Conn. [See below.]

Lucy Thurston, daughter of Worthington Buckley and Jane Cellina (Allen) Button, was born June 28, 1852, at New London, Conn. ; she was baptized in her infancy by the Rev. Dr. Hallam, in St. James' Church. She was married in New York City, by the Rev. Charles W. Palmer, December 27, 1876, to James Cornelius Church (son of Cornelius Church). James C. Church was born November 10, 1850, at South Scituate, Mass. He was graduated at the St. Lawrence University, of New York, in 1874; he was ordained in the Congregational Church, at Gill, Mass., June 13, 1878. The children of Lucy Thurston (Button) and James Cornelius Church were :

1 Lucy Allen, born October 23, 1877, at the Parsonage at Gill, Mass.; she was baptized by her father, at his first Communion after his ordination.
2 Maud Birchard, born June 9, 1879, at the Parsonage at Gill, Mass. ; she was baptized by her father at his last administration of the Holy Communion in that place.
3 James Worthington, born October 23, 1882, at Hampton, Conn.; died February 5, 1888. He was baptized at the old homestead, in Hampton, Conn., three days before his death ; he was a noble boy. The service was very impressive, the Rev. Daniel Denison officiating.
4 Daisy Thurston, born September 15, 1884, at Hampton, Conn. " For Lucy Allen and Daisy Thurston we have this blessed hope, that the first sound that breaks the long silence to them may be the welcome home from their Saviour's voice."
5 Annie Hortense, born February 25, 1886, at Hampton, Conn. Daisy Thurston and Annie Hortense were baptized at the same time, February 2, 1888, with their loved brother.
6 Miriam Worthington, born Thursday, November 12, 1891, at Brookline, Mass.

Eleanor Caroline, sixth daughter and ninth child of Lewis and Mary Denison Allen, was born April 29, 1828, at New London, Conn. ; she was baptized in infancy, by the Rev. Bethel Judd, D. D., Rector of St. James' Church, New London, Conn. She was married to William, son of Dr. Archibald and Harriet (Wheat) Mercer, September 13, 1847. William Mercer was born at New London, Conn., March 21, 1821. When quite young he was in the dry goods business in that city; afterwards in Buffalo, N. Y., and in Indiana. The marriage ceremony took place at her father's, the Rev. Dr. Hallam officiating. William Mercer died in Indiana, April 22, 1871, aged 50 years, 1 month, and 1 day. His widow, with their six children, returned to New London, Conn., to reside, but is now (1891) at Los Angelos, Cal. The children of Eleanor C. and William Mercer were :

1 Mary Stoddard, born August 12, 1849, at Buffalo, N. Y.; she died November 15, 1854.
2 Archibald, born March 23, 1851, at Buffalo, N. Y.
3 William Allen, born March 19, 1855, at Buffalo, N. Y. He married July 2, 1877. [See below.]
4 Thomas Allen, born April 6, 1857, at Buffalo, N. Y.; died January 17, 1858.
5 John Derhen, born February 8, 1859, in Indiana.
6 Ellen Allen, born July 15, 1860, in Indiana.
7 Harriet, born November 24, 1862, in Indiana.
8 Frederick Worthington, born June 24, 1865, in Indiana. He married Statira Lavinia Palmer, in New London, on Tuesday, March 5, 1889, the Rev. A. Douglas Miller, former Rector of St. James' Church, officiating. They have one child, Eleanor Palmer Mercer, born September 26, 1890, in New London, Conn.

William Allen, second son of William and Eleanor Caroline (Allen) Mercer, was born at Buffalo, N. Y., March 19, 1855; he was baptized by the Rev. Edward Ingersoll, D. D., in Trinity Church, Buffalo, N. Y., and confirmed by the Right Rev. Joseph Cruikshank Talbot, in Christ Church, Indianapolis, Ind., on Easter Day, April 9, 1871. He married Carrie Louise Meeker, July 2, 1877, in New London, Conn., the Rev. William Byron Buckingham, Rector of St. James' Church, officiating. She was born August 12, 1858. They had two children :

1 William Allen, born April 16, 1878, at New London, Conn.; died August 24, 1878. He was baptized by the Rev. William B. Buckingham, at St. James'.

2 Edith Wait, born April 19, 1881, at Columbus, O.; she was baptized by the Rev. L. Delos Mansfield, at Benecia, Cal.

William Allen Mercer was appointed Second Lieutenant in the 8th United States Infantry, November, 1880; he was on duty at Columbus Barracks, O., December, 1880, to April, 1881; at Fort Yuma, Cal., from April 23, 1881, to September 3 following; in the field against hostile Apache Indians, in Arizona, September 3 to December 20, 1881; at Benecia Barracks, Cal., December, 1881, to May, 1882; Fort McDermit, Nev., May 5, 1882, to September 16, 1882; again at Benecia Barracks, Cal., to June, 1883; at United States Infantry and Cavalry School, Fort Leavenworth, Kan., June, 1883, to June, 1885; Fort McDermit, Nev., June, 1885, to June, 1886; Fort Grant, Arizona Territory, July 8, 1886; in the field against hostile Indians, Arizona, to November 25, 1886; at Fort Robinson, Neb., December 1, 1886, to September 1, 1890, when the Company was disbanded. He was appointed First Lieutenant March 9, 1889. He was stationed at Fort Niobrara, Neb., March, 1889, to November, 1890; on field service against Sioux Indians, from November 19, 1890, to January 28, 1891, in South Dakota; at Fort McKinney, Wyoming, from February 10, 1891, to date (July, 1891). He was appointed Regimental Quartermaster, June 30, 1891, and assigned to duty, as Post Quartermaster, at Fort McKinney. He obtained the "Distinguished Marksman's Medal" in 1889.

RECORD OF THE FAMILY OF WILLIAM, SON OF THOMAS AND AMELIA (TABER) ALLEN.*

William Allen, third son of Thomas and Amelia (Taber) Allen, was born March 13, 1785, on his father's farm, called the Mount Pleasant estate, near New London, Conn. He was baptized by the Right Rev. Samuel Seabury, D. D., and confirmed by the Right Rev. Abraham Jarvis, in 1800, in St. James' Church, New London, Conn. When eight years old he went with his parents to live on Fisher's Island, N. Y. In 1812 he moved with them to Pomfret, Conn. He married, January 18, 1815, at Trinity Church, Brooklyn, Conn, Emily Chandler, the eldest child of John Wilkes and Mary Chandler, the Rev. Daniel Fogg, D. D., performing the ceremony. The bride was dressed in a dark blue riding-habit, or dress. Her bridesmaids were Elizabeth and Frances Taber Allen, sisters of the bridegroom.

William Allen was a man of noble and commanding presence (over six feet in height). The bridal pair rode to the church in a chaise; Capt. Thomas Allen, Jr., with his wife and their daughters (the parents and sisters of the bridegroom) following in their coach; Mr. George Bowen and his wife came to the wedding from Woodstock, Conn., in a coach; Mr. Pardon Tillinghast Taber (uncle of the bridegroom) and his wife, Mr. John Griffing and Capt. Thomas Wilson, came from New London that day — the last two riding fleet horses and arriving just in time. Mr. Charles Grosvenor and members of the Chandler family were also present.

After the ceremony, Mrs. Chandler entertained them all at her house in Pomfret, where they doubtless had a jolly time. There the bride wore a white satin dress, satin slippers, a pearl band in her hair, and a pearl girdle around her waist. It was said by those present, that they never saw a fairer, sweeter, or more lovely bride. The next day the newly married couple went to Capt. Thomas Allen's house, where they

---

* See page 37.

remained a short time. William and Emily (Chandler) Allen began housekeeping on the smaller, or 280 acre Nightingale Farm, where he built a nice house, which is now (1891) in good repair.

Mrs. William Allen was baptized in her own house, with her son, William Arthur Wellesley, a babe six months old, by the Rev. Ashbel Steele, Rector of Trinity Church, Brooklyn, Conn. Miss Betsey Putnam (daughter of Col. Putnam), of Brooklyn, was present, and probably one of the sponsors. Mrs. Allen was confirmed in Christ Church, Pomfret, July 20, 1834, by the Right Rev. Thomas Church Brownell.

After the death of her husband (who died of dropsy in the chest, March 20, 1833, aged 47 years, 11 months and 24 days, at Rope Ferry, East Lyme, where they had lived three or four years), she returned to Pomfret with eight children. Her tenth child was born the following September. Mrs. Allen spent the last fifteen years of her life at her daughter's (Mrs. Leonard Ames) in Oswego, N. Y. She died April 26, 1882, the day of her grand-daughter's marriage — a sad anniversary to all. She was a lovely Christian woman. She was born in Pomfret, Conn., September 8, 1793, and had reached the age of 88 years, 7 months and 14 days, when she left for Paradise. The children of William and Emily Allen were :

1 William Arthur Wellesley, born May 10, 1816, at Pomfret ; he died in 1853. [See below.]

2 Henry Hobart, born August, 1817, at Pomfret ; he only lived twelve hours.

3 Horatio Nelson, born November 20, 1818, at Pomfret. [See below.]

4 Mary Chandler, born October 17, 1820 ; she was married September 20, 1841. [See below.]

5 Martha Helen, born July 11, 1822, at Pomfret ; she was married March 24, 1842. [See below.]

6 Nathaniel Hamilton, born August 24, 1824, at Pomfret ; died December 5, 1845, in Boston.

7 John Chandler, born August 26, 1826, at Pomfret ; married June 3, 1852. [See below.]

WILLIAM ALLEN.

MRS. EMILY (CHANDLER) ALLEN.

HON. CALEB JOHNSON ALLEN.

JAMES A. ALLEN.

8 Anna Maria, born July 12, 1828 ; she was married January 9, 1856. [See below.]

9 Sarah Shannon, born November 27, 1830, at Rope Ferry ; she was married September 6, 1882. [See below.]

10 Emma, born September 13, 1833 ; she was married July 7, 1868, at Pomfret ; died at Worcester, February 26, 1892, at ten, P. M. ; buried at Worcester.

William Arthur Wellesley Allen, eldest son of William and Emily (Chandler) Allen, married Maria Bixby ; they had one child, a son, named William. The father died in California, in 1853 ; since then nothing has been heard of Mrs. Maria (Bixby) Allen, or her son.

Horatio Nelson, third son of William and Emily (Chandler) Allen, was born in Pomfret, Conn., November 20, 1818, and was baptized in infancy. He was a clerk in the Post Office, in New London, Conn., three or four years. He married Lucy H. Bullock, at Williamsburg, Long Island, N. Y. The children of Horatio Nelson and Lucy H. (Bullock) Allen were :

1 Henry Nelson, born January 21, 1852, at Williamsburg, N. Y.

2 Francis W., born September 9, 1853 ; married in 1880.

3 Jesse Bullock, born January 10, 1855, at Mexico, N. Y. ; married in 1880.

4 Leonard Ames, born in 1856, at Rockford, Ill.

5 Lucretia Cordelia, born February 28, 1858, at Rockford. She died July 6, 1858.

6 Horatio Chandler, born in 1860, at Rockford.

7 Helen Chandler, born April 22, 1865, at Rockford.

Mary Chandler, eldest daughter of William and Emily (Chandler) Allen, was born on the Nightingale Farm, in Pomfret, Conn,, October 7, 1820. She was married at Mexico, N. Y., September 20, 1841, to Charles Loring Webb, son of Loring and Judith (Pratt) Webb. He was born August 6, 1816, and died November 5, 1885, aged 69 years, 2 months and 29 days. He was for some time a merchant in Mexico,

N. Y. ; afterwards he was appointed Purser in the United States Navy. The children of Charles L. and Mary C. (Allen) Webb, who were all born at Mexico, N. Y., were :

1 Marian Holt, born November 10, 1842. [See below.]
2 Edward Gerry, born August 16, 1846 ; died, aged six months, in 1847.
3 Adelaide Emily, born December 27, 1847. [See below.]
4 Edward Gerry, born April 3, 1850. [See below.]
5 Sarah Allen, born March 15, 1852. [See below.]
6 George Chandler, born February 15, 1854. [See below.]
7 Annie Ames, born April 4, 1856. [See below.]
8 Theodore Herbert, born April 17, 1858. [See below.]
9 Josephine Rose, born September 16, 1860 ; died October 6, 1870.

Marian Holt, eldest daughter of Charles Loring and Mary C. (Allen) Webb, was born November 10, 1842 ; she was married to Andrew Johnson, a lawyer, at Mexico, N. Y., December 26, 1863. Their children are :

1 Mary Grace, born April 2, 1867.
2 Addie Estelle, born May 1, 1871.
3 George Webb, born ——
4 Charles Webb, born ——

Adelaide Emily, second daughter of Charles Loring and Mary C. (Allen) Webb, was born at Mexico, N. Y., December 27, 1847. She was married, first, to John Henry Alfred, September 29, 1880 ; he died February 12, 1881. Her second husband was George H. Goodwin ; they were married June 5, 1883, and had one child, Mabel Adelaide Goodwin, who died when six months old. Mrs. Adelaide Emily (Webb) Goodwin died April 14, 1884, aged 36 years, 3 months and 18 days.

Edward Gerry, second of the name, and eldest son who lived to manhood, of Charles Loring and Mary C. (Allen) Webb, was born April 3, 1852. He married September 4, 1872, at Mexico, N. Y., Imogene Manley. Their children are Charles Manley ; Edward Boomer ; and Theodore Allen Webb.

Sarah Allen, third daughter of Charles Loring and Mary C. (Allen) Webb, was born March 15, 1852 ; she was married to George P. Johnson, M. D., June 5, 1883, at Mexico, N. Y. They have one child, Fannie.

George Chandler, third son and sixth child of Charles Loring and Mary C. (Allen) Webb, was born February 15, 1854 ; he married January 24, 1884, Charlotte Lansing Boyd. Their children are Manette Boyd ; Henry Chandler ; and George Chandler Webb, Jr.

Annie Ames, fourth daughter of Charles Loring and Mary C. (Allen) Webb, was born April 4, 1856 ; she was married at Mexico, N. Y., February 8, 1881, to Frank Myers Tracy. They have no children.

Theodore Herbert, youngest son of Charles Loring and Mary C. (Allen) Webb, was born April 17, 1858 ; he married in Mexico, N. Y., Elizabeth Smith, November 14, 1883. They have no children.

Martha Helen, second daughter of William and Emily (Chandler) Allen, was born on the Nightingale place, Pomfret, Conn., July 11, 1822 ; she was baptized in her infancy. She was married March 24, 1842, in Pomfret, Conn., to William Henry Chandler, who was born in Providence, R. I., April 27, 1816 ; he was graduated at Yale College, August 24, 1839, and died in Thompson, Conn., May 13, 1888. The children of Martha Helen (Allen) and William Henry Chandler were all born in Thompson, and were :

1 Charlotte Helen, born October 10, 1843 ; she was married to George Luther Whitman, of New York, March 31, 1868.
2 Harriet Tisdale, born April 1, 1846 ; married Charles Robert Forrest, October 15, 1868.
3 Randolph William, born September 24, 1848 ; died August 24, 1852.
4 Sarah Backus, born August 2, 1850 ; died June 17, 1851.

5 Randolph Henry, born July 11, 1853; married December 23, 1886, Dora Aldrich, of Woodstock, Conn. He is an attorney-at-law, in Putnam, Conn.

6 Sarah Hodges, born June 23, 1855; she was married September 28, 1881, to John Boswell, of New York City.

7 Emily Allen, born December 24, 1857; she was married June 5, 1879, to Charles Hubbell, of New York.

John Chandler, fifth son and seventh child of William and Emily (Chandler) Allen, was born on the Nightingale farm, in Pomfret, Conn., August 26, 1826. He was baptized in his infancy. When he was about six and a half years old his father died, and he went soon after, to reside with his uncle, John Chandler, (his mother's brother, for whom he was named) in the State of New York. His uncle died, and he married Marianne Hitchcock (the Rev. William Van Valkenburg, officiating), at Annville, N. Y., June 3, 1852. Marianne Hitchcock was born at Westerloo, N. Y., April 18, 1825. After his marriage he moved to Rockford, Ill., and from there to Central City, Kan., and subsequently to Olympia, Wash., where he died January 24, 1889, aged 62 years, 4 months and 29 days. The children of John Chandler and Marianne (Hitchcock) Allen, were:

1 Alice Elizabeth, born November 16, 1855, at Rockford, Ill.

2 Edward Chandler, born June 1, 1858, at Milford, Ill.; died July, 1859.

3 Charles Frederick, born May 14, 1859, at Milford, Ill.; married December 22, 1887.

4 Lydia Emily, born August 5, 1861, at Rockford, Ill.; married September 8, 1886.

5 Sarah Amelia, born August 6. 1863, at Big Foot Corners, Walworth Co., Wis.

6 Arthur Wellesley, born February 8, 1866, at Central City, Kan.; died September, 1866.

7 Lillian May, born March 26, 1868, at Central City, Kan.; died April 3, 1868.

Charles Frederick, second son of John Chandler and Marianne (Hitchcock) Allen, born May 14, 1859; married Rose May Ward, at Edna, Kan., December 22, 1887. He is a merchant. They have one child, Hazel Chandler, born at Olympia, Wash., December 3, 1888.

Lydia Emily, second daughter of John Chandler and Marianne (Hitchcock) Allen, was born August 5, 1861; she was married to Royal B. McCausland (a merchant), September 8, 1886, at Olympia, Wash. They have two children:

1 Cally, born July 20, 1887.
2 Harold Allen, born July 16, 1888.

Anna Maria, third daughter of William and Emily (Chandler) Allen, was born on the Nightingale farm, in Pomfret, Conn., July 13, 1828; she was baptized by the Rev. Ezra B. Kellogg, and confirmed by the Right Rev. Arthur Cleveland Coxe, D. D., LL. D., in Christ Church, Oswego, N. Y., 1865. She was married January 9, 1856, by the Rev. Thomas Weed, of Mexico, N. Y., to Leonard Ames, who was born at Mexico, N. Y., February 8, 1818. He was a banker in that place; he is now a resident of Oswego, and in business there. The children of Anna Maria (Allen) and Leonard Ames, are:

1 Allen, born October 23, 1859, at Mexico, N. Y.; baptized by the Rev. Alfred B. Beach, D. D.
2 Fannie Chandler, born July 5, 1861, at Mexico, N. Y.; baptized by the same clergyman.
3 Alfred Howlett, born March 6, 1867, at Oswego, N. Y.; he was baptized by the Rev. Dr. Beach.

Allen and Fannie were confirmed in Christ Church, Oswego, N. Y., by the Right Rev. Arthur Cleveland Coxe, Bishop of Western New York. Fannie Chandler Ames was married in Christ Church, Oswego, April 26, 1882, by the Rev. Dr. Beach, to Leonard Hiram Dewing, who was born at New York City, November 13, 1858. They have one child, Harold Ames, born March 22, 1884, at Hartford, Conn.; he was baptized by the Rev. Dr. E. P. Parker, Pastor of the South Congregational Church of Hartford. Allen and Alfred How- lett Ames are partners with their half-brother, Leonard Ames, Jr., in the Ames Iron Works, in Oswego, N. Y.

Sarah Shannon, fourth daughter of William and Emily (Chandler) Allen, was born November 27, 1830, at Rope Ferry (Niantic Bar), at what is now known as East Lyme, Conn. The property was originally owned by Major Edward Palmer, a son-in-law of Governor Winthrop, of that Colony. After her father's death she went with her mother to Pomfret, Conn., where she was baptized by the Rev. Ezra B. Kellogg, Rector of Christ Church. She was married September 6, 1882, to Mr. John Burrows, of Mexico, N. Y. The ceremony took place at the residence of her brother-in-law, Mr. Leonard Ames, in Oswego, N. Y., the Rev. D. Tully, officiating. John Burrows was born January 30, 1819, in Middletown, Conn.; he was the son of John and Margaret (Braddock) Burrows. Mr. Burrows entered the U. S. Naval Service, August 7, 1845, and was with Commodore Robert F. Stockton, in the Frigate Congress, during the Mexican War; he assisted in the taking of California; he was appointed a boatswain in the Navy, December 4, 1849; he served on the Wachusett in the War of the Rebellion, and was with Capt. Collins, when he took the Confederate steamer Florida from under the forts in Bahia, Brazil. He was placed on the "Retired List," Janu- ary 30, 1881.

Emma, youngest daughter of William and Emily (Chandler) Allen, was born at Pomfret, Conn., September 13, 1833; she was baptized when an infant by the Rev. Ezra B. Kellogg, the Rector, in Christ Church. She was confirmed in All Saints', Worcester, Mass., by Right Rev. Manton Eastburn, March 11, 1863. She was married in Christ Church, Pom- fret, (the same Church where she was baptized) by the Rev. John Gilliat, July 7, 1868, to Albert Wood, M. D. Dr. Wood was born in Northboro', Mass., February 19, 1833. He was a descendant of William Wood, who emigrated to New England in 1638, at the age of 56 years, and settled at Concord, Mass., where he died May 14, 1671, aged 89 years. His son Michael Wood died at Concord, Mass., May 13, 1674. His son Abraham removed to Sudbury and his son Samuel lived in that part of Marlboro', now Northboro'. Abraham married Lydia Johnson, and their son Samuel, born February 22, 1799, was found dead in his bed, Monday morning, November 10, 1879, having attended church the day before. Samuel Wood married Elizabeth Bowman. Their son, Dr. Albert Wood, is a graduate of the Scientific Department of Dartmouth College, in 1856; he received the degree of M. D. at Harvard College in 1862; he was First Assistant Surgeon of the 29th Massachusetts Regiment Infantry, and was promoted to be Surgeon of the 1st Massachusetts Cavalry, August 7, 1863. He was City Physician and Surgeon at Worcester, Mass., 1870–4, and was the first person to present a practical plan to the City Council, for the establishment of a City Hospital in Worcester. His plan was accepted, and the Hospital opened in 1874. Dr. Wood was, at first, one of the physicians, and afterwards surgeon of the Hospital, until June, 1886, when he resigned, having been elected a Trustee of the institution. He has been Treasurer of the Worcester Hospital for the Chronic Insane, for many years. He is also Trustee of the Memorial Hospital. He started the Washburn Free Dispensary, and performed the duties of Superintendent for twelve years. He is now one of the Board of Examining Surgeons for Pensions, at Worcester, Mass. Mrs. Emma A. Wood died in Worcester, February 26, 1892; she was buried the 29th of February, at 3.30, P. M., in Rural Cemetery, Worcester, Mass. The children of Dr. Albert and Emma (Allen) Wood are :

1 Albert Bowman, born June 28, 1869. Now a student at Harvard College.

2 Emily Chandler, born April 24, 1873.

Frances Taber, second daughter of Thomas and Amelia (Taber) Allen, was born in what was called the Goshen house,

Great Neck, New London, Conn., at 6 o'clock, on Wednesday morning, March 21, 1787. She went with her parents, April 1, 1793, to live on Fisher's Island, N. Y., when she was six years old, and resided there nineteen years. She was confirmed by the Right Rev. Abraham Jarvis, in 1800, in St. James' Church, New London, Conn. She moved with her parents to Pomfret, Conn., April 1, 1812; they lived on the Nightingale farm. She was married July 26, 1815, in St. James' Church, New London, at six o'clock in the morning, by the Rev. Solomon Blakesley, Rector of St. James, to Jesse Denison Smith, to whom she had been engaged seven years. Jesse D. Smith was born in Stonington (Wickutequock), October 10, 1783. He was baptized July 13, 1788. He was the fourteenth child of Col. Oliver and Mary (Denison) Smith. At the wedding, the bride was dressed in white satin, and white slippers, and wore a white satin bonnet; after the ceremony they had a wedding breakfast at her uncle's; then, attired in a dark green ladies-cloth habit, she rode in a chaise to Pomfret, with her husband, where her parents gave a reception for them. They would have been married in Trinity Church, Brooklyn, Conn., had not the Rev. Daniel Fogg, who had been Rector many years, died just before, and the Parish was without a Rector.

Frances Taber (Allen) and Jesse Denison Smith had but one child, Frances Mary, born July 30, 1816; baptized by the Rev. Solomon Blakesley, Rector of St. James' Church, New London, Conn., September, 1816. She was confirmed by the Right Rev. Thomas Church Brownell, in Christ Church, Pomfret, Conn., August 2, 1835. She received her first Communion on the Nightingale farm, the home of her aged grandparents, Thomas and Amelia (Taber) Allen. They received with her together with her mother, Mrs. Frances Taber (Allen) Smith, and her aunts, Elizabeth and Amelia Allen. The Rev. Ezra B. Kellogg was celebrant; it was a very solemn service. All who were present, except the writer, are now (I fully believe), in Paradise.

JESSE DENISON SMITH.

MRS. FRANCES TABER (ALLEN) SMITH.

MRS. FRANCES MARY (SMITH) BOLLES.

WILLIAM CAREY BOLLES.

Frances Mary Smith was married to William Carey Bolles, second son of Rev. Lucius Bolles, D. D., and his wife Lydia, November 22, 1841, by the Rev. Robert A. Hallam, D. D., Rector, in St. James' Church, New London, Conn., at 12 o'clock, noon. This was the first wedding but one, and that soon after, since the bride's parents were married in that Church. The bells rang for twelve as the bridal party entered the Church, and a merry wedding peal as they came out. The bride was dressed in a silver gray pelisse, a bonnet of white watered silk, with long white feather and a short veil. She had an informal reception at her aunt's (Stanton Place), and in the evening at her cousin's (Jonathan Starr), a very handsome one. Her uncle (Lewis Allen), who gave away the bride, gave a dinner-party for the bride and groom the next day, and after dinner, they, with their bridesmaids and groomsmen, her mother and other relatives (twelve in all) in three carriages, drove to Norwich, Conn., and took the train to Pomfret, where they had still another reception, at the bride's grandfather's, — a merry time for all. On November 25, Thanksgiving Day, they arrived in Boston, and dined at his father's, the Rev. Lucius Bolles, D. D., who gave a reception, early in December, for his son William Carey Bolles, and his bride.

The father of Jesse Denison Smith (husband of Frances Taber Allen), was a merchant, and also engaged in commerce, owning a large number of vessels. His mother died when he was seventeen years old, and, soon after, Jesse began a sea-faring life. In 1810 he left New York for the East Indies, as first officer on board a packet ship, owned by Minturn & Champlaine. The ship was taken by the Danes, and carried into Gottenburg, where it was kept sixteen months, and then condemned. He next served as first officer on board the brig Comet, Capt. John Dennis, master, but while at Kiel, in February, 1813, he learned of the War of 1812, and resolved to take an active part in it. Accordingly he took charge of fifty men, and travelled to Paris (about 1700 miles) to join the

True Blooded Yankee, an American privateer owned by
Mr. Preble, of Boston, Mass.   "She was manned by a crew of
about two hundred men, and carried sixteen guns.   Preble
was at that time residing in Paris.   Near the time Capt.
Smith arrived in Kiel, the ship Integrity had been captured
by the True Blooded Yankee, and sent to Norway.   It is
not unlikely that the prize crew, which brought this ship into
port, were turned over to Capt. Smith, and are the men who
travelled with him to rejoin their vessel in France."

His account with the owner of the privateer begins in
August, 1813, with the entry, "By cash received from Mr.
Forbes, in Copenhagen, 4350 Danish dollars;" he also received
money at other places on his journey.   The accounts of
expenses for the fifty men were very carefully kept, and
included such items as "lost in exchange, signing passports,
and guide, lodging, coffee, breakfast for all hands, post wagons,
two days' provision, etc."   The route taken was from Copenhagen by sail to Sonderburg, and thence to Altona, where they
arrived August 8, 1813 ; then by boat from Hamburg to Har-
burg ; thence overland by wagons, through the following
places : Torshine, Rotenburg, Otterberg, Bremen, Delmen-
horst, Oldenburg, Burford, Grootzundet, Leer and Winschoten ;
thence by boat across the Ems river and canal to Groningen
and on to Strolos, Lammer, Amsterdam, Rotterdam, Antwerp
and Paris.   Here he joined the True Blooded Yankee, as
Prize-master, Thomas Oxnard, of Boston, being Captain.

In alluding to this astonishing vessel, Coggeshall, in his
"History of American Privateers," says : "She had been
thirty-seven days at sea, during which she captured twenty-
seven vessels, and made 270 prisoners, going into France with
one cargo worth $400,000, some of the items being 18 bales
of Turkey carpets, 12,000 pounds raw silk, 2,000 swan skins,
etc."   Capt. Smith, as Prize-master, carried one of the prizes
into France, but while going in with the second one assigned
to him, he was captured by a British cruiser, and kept for a
time by the officers, who told him if he would stay with them

until the end of the war, he should fare as well as they did ; but he chose to be sent to England. The old ship, Queen Charlotte, came with provisions, wood and water, and he went in her ; but instead of being exchanged, as he expected to be, he was sent to Plymouth, England, and from there to Dartmoor Prison. As he was a single man, and his father and mother were both dead, the first news that his family received of his imprisonment was by a letter to his brother, Denison Smith (then a merchant at Groton, Conn.), post-marked Boston, September 7, 1814. I give a copy of that letter.

DARTMOOR, June 15, 1814.

DEAR BROTHER :

I embrace the first opportunity of writing you, to inform you of my welfare, since I left you in America. After my ship was condemned in Norway, I shipped on board a brig bound to (torn off) via Kiel ; arrived safe in Kiel, but there heard of the War. I was discharged from the brig, took charge of 50 men and joined the True Blooded Yankee in France, as Prize-master. I made three safe cruises in her, and went in safe in one of the prizes, but on the last cruise took a rich prize and I was put in her ; but was captured by the Sea Horse Frigate, on March 22, 1814, and brought to England, where I must remain, until peace or an exchange.

I have much prize money due, to the amount of $3,000, but do not expect to obtain it before my release : it is, I think, in safe hands, but yours would be preferable.

I cannot but recall to remembrance with pleasure, the many happy scenes we have had together in Groton. I have hopes still of enjoying some more happy days together, but when, God knows. I have with a great deal of sorrow, received the news of the death of our respected father, and beloved brother Edward. I sincerely deplore their loss, as our father was a kind and indulgent one, and Edward a beloved brother ; I regret that I did not take a last farewell of them, but God's will be done. I hope you have enjoyed a good state of health and still enjoy it, and beg leave to be, dear brother, sincerely and affectionately, yours truly,

JESSE D. SMITH.

P. S.   Give my compliments to all of your family and the rest of our relatives, and give my best respects to Miss Allen, if unmarried and you think proper.   J. D. S.

Jesse D. Smith requested his brother, Denison Smith, to direct his letters to Dartmoor Prison, Devonshire, England. He was released in May, 1815, having made three unsuccessful attempts to escape.   He arrived in New York during the next month.

Capt. Smith married Frances Taber Allen, the lady referred to in his letter, on July 26, 1815.   On December 22, 1815, he was in a rigging loft in New York City, giving directions to his men, when just at dark, he mistook the hatchway for the stairway and fell fifteen feet, striking on a hogshead of sugar. He was carried to the Marine hospital (after being robbed of his watch and money), arriving there at 12 o'clock, where he remained insensible, or nearly so, for ten days; he was there seven weeks in all.   His limbs never recovered their elasticity, and that probably caused, some time after, another fall, by which he lost his life.

His wife was at her father's in Pomfret, at the time of his accident, but as soon as informed of it, left home, and was one week going from New London to New York, in a packet-ship, arriving January 1, 1816.   As soon as he was able, they returned to New London, Conn., where he remained the most of the time until April, 1817.   He then sailed to New York, and from there went in the brig Wrangler to the Mediterranean Sea.   He stopped at Leghorn and then went to Trieste, where they sold the brig, and he took passage on board the ship Beulah, Captain Williams, of Boston.   On November 4, 1817, Capt. Smith volunteered to go aloft in a severe storm, to take in sail.   The masts were covered with ice and he fell from the masthead, and went overboard; every effort was made to save him, but in vain.   Capt. Williams wrote that he thought he struck on his head in his fall, and was unable to help himself; they heard him groan, but it being dark, could not see him. He was only thirty-four years old, a noble and very generous man, beloved by all who knew him.

He became a communicant of the Protestant Episcopal Church, in 1816, and received his first Communion in St. James' Church, New London, Conn., — the same Church in which he was married in 1815, and where his wife Frances Taber (Allen) was confirmed, and where their only child was married, November 22, 1841, to William Carey Bolles, by the Rev. Robert A. Hallam, D. D.

Capt. Jesse D. Smith was a descendant of Rev. Nehemiah Smith, who came to Boston, New England, July 26, 1637, and who married Sarah Ann, a daughter of the first Thomas Bourne, of Marshfield, and his wife Elizabeth, January 21, 1640. They moved from Marshfield to Stratford, Conn., and from there to New Haven, where their son Nehemiah, 2d, was born, and baptized October 24, 1646, by the Rev. John Davenport. He moved with his father to Pequonnoc farm, adjoining Smith Lake, when he was ten years of age. When he was seventeen years old, if not earlier, his father was living in Norwich, Conn., having left him on the homestead. At twenty-three, he married (October 24, 1669), Lydia Winchester, of Roxbury, Mass. During that year he was a member of the General Assembly, at Hartford, Conn., which office he held in several subsequent years. By his father's will, he received the title to the Pequonnoc farm, since known as the Smith homestead. He bought a large tract of land at Niantic, Conn., in 1691–2. This land was known as the Soldiers' Land.*

The following is the blazon of the arms of the Smyth or Smith Family, 1561, which have been preserved in this branch of their descendants ; their conection with the ancestry of the Rev. Nehemiah Smith, the first settler, is traditional.

---

* See Genealogical History of the Descendants of Rev. Nehemiah Smith, by H. Allen Smith, of Brooklyn, New York.

Gules two bars wavy ermine ; on a chief or, a demi lion rampant, sable, crowned or.   Crest, A tiger passant argent, vulned on the shoulder proper.   The motto, if any, has not been preserved.

It was assigned to John Smyth in 1561, at Newcastle-under-Lyne, County of Stafford.   (Smith of Elmhurst and Stafford County.)   John Smith was the second son of the Right Rev. Dr. Smith, Bishop of Litchfield and Coventry, whose great-grandson, John Smith, Esq., of Heath-End House, near Newcastle-under-Lyne, was living at the Visitation in 1614, and had his arms confirmed there.

Rev. Nehemiah (the first of the name), died in Norwich, Conn., about 1686, aged (about) 81 years ; his wife (Sarah Ann Bourne), born about 1615, died after January 12, 1684. They were both buried in the Post and Gager burying-ground, in Norwich, in the oldest part of the cemetery.   All the early residents were buried there, and all without stones to mark the exact place of their graves.   A granite monument which contains the name of Nehemiah Smith, and other proprietors, has been erected on the highest portion of the ground.

Nehemiah, 2d, died August 8, 1727, aged 83 years and 9 months.   His wife, Lydia, died October 24, 1723, in the seventieth year of her age.   Nehemiah Smith, 3d, was born on the Smith homestead, November 14, 1673.   He married, April 22, 1696, Dorothy Wheeler, a daughter of Isaac and Martha (Park) Wheeler.   She was born December 6, 1679, and died May 25, 1736.   Nehemiah, 3d, died November 21, 1724, when fifty-one years of age.   They had twelve children.   He was born and always resided on the homestead.   He was Townsman in 1712-14, and was highly respected.   He and his wife are buried in Smith Lake Cemetery, Pequonnoc.   Their son Nathan, born at the Smith homestead, September 16, 1702, married Mary Denison, of Stonington, December 5, 1723 (the Rev. Ebenezer Rossiter officiating).   She was a sister of his brother Isaac's wife, and the daughter of Deacon Daniel and Mary (Stanton) Denison.*

Less than a year after his marriage his father died, leaving him, at the age of twenty-two, in charge of the homestead farm, which was a very large one. His house was burned, and with it many papers and books, valuable as containing family history. He rebuilt over the same cellar, and this dwelling is still standing, and is now owned by one of his great-great-grandsons, Jabez Smith. Nathan spent his entire life of eighty-two years on the farm. He died December 4, 1784, and his wife, with whom he had lived sixty-one years, died February 20, 1793, aged 87 years. They are buried in Smith Lake Cemetery.

Their son Oliver was born at the Smith homestead, April 27, 1739, in the first house, built about 1653. Oliver married April 5, 1759, Mary Denison, a daughter of John and Mary (Noyes) Denison, and a descendant of William Denison, who came to America from England, in 1631. She was also a descendant of John Howland, a passenger on the Mayflower in 1620. Mrs. Smith was the mother of sixteen children; two of them died in infancy, three died when between twenty and twenty-three years of age; eleven married and had children. Mary (Denison) Smith died September 17, 1800, in the fifty-ninth year of her age.

Col. Oliver, and his wife, Mary (Denison) Smith, moved from Groton to Stonington, Conn., in the spring of 1761. He was fully six feet in height and well-proportioned; he had dark eyes, and in the later years of his life, his hair, which he retained till his death, was grey. He was naturally straight, and in walking showed a military bearing; gentlemanly in his manner, he enjoyed entertaining his friends at his home. Gen. Washington occasionally called upon him, and he named his tenth child George Washington, as the General was at the house soon after his birth, January 16, 1776. The

---

* See Descendants of George Denison, p. 121.

Colonel was very fond of music, and was himself a violinist above the ordinary ability of amateurs. Early in the War of the Revolution, and on August 30, 1775, he was Captain of a Company stationed at Stonington Long Point, when the British ship Rose, in command of Capt. Wallace, bombarded the village. Capt. Smith was promoted to be Major soon after that event, and on July 3, 1776, he was promoted to the rank of Colonel. He died August 1, 1811, in the seventy-third year of his age. Both he and his wife are buried in Smith Lake Cemetery, Pequonnoc, Conn.

THE BOLLES FAMILY.

THE Family of Bolles was originally from Bolle Hall and Hough, in the County of Lincoln, England. The senior branch of the family enjoyed the title of Baronet until 1700, when the Bolles line of Scampton became extinct in Sir Richard Bolles, Baronet.

ARMS OF THE BOLLES FAMILY.

Azure, three boar's heads, argent, out of three cups, or. Crest, A demi wild boar, rampant, wounded in the breast with a broken tilting spear, all proper (or natural) colors. Motto, En Dieu est ma fiance. [In God is my trust.]

It is said that " The three cups signify the Church, having an allusion to the Trinity; the boar's heads show courage in defence of religion. The crest signifies that the original bearer had been wounded whilst acting with great courage in defence of his country."

The Rev. Lucius Bolles, D. D., was the fourth son of David and Susanna (Moor) Bolles. He was born at Ashford, Conn., September 25, 1779; he was graduated at Brown University, Providence, R. I., in 1801 ; he was Curator of the University from 1807 to 1818. The degree of D. D. or S. T. D., was conferred upon him by Union College, Schenectady, N. Y., in 1824. He was Pastor of the First Baptist Church, in Salem, Mass., from its foundation, in December, 1804, for

REV. LUCIUS BOLLES, D. D.

MRS. LYDIA BOLLES.

MRS. FRANCES AMELIA (BOLLES) PATTERSON.

REV. GEORGE HERBERT PATTERSON.

20 years. He resigned that position to become Corresponding Secretary of the Baptist Board of Foreign Missions, which office he held for nearly eighteen years.

He married his cousin Lydia, daughter of John and Lydia (Taber) Bolles, September 8, 1805, in Hartford, Conn., where she was born October 10, 1784, and died there June 20, 1851. The Rev. Dr. Bolles died of consumption, January 5, 1844, at his home in Boston. He had the confidence and respect of all who knew him, and left his memory enshrined in the warmest affections of the heart. He and his wife were buried in the Bolles lot, at Mount Auburn Cemetery, Cambridge. Lucius and Lydia Bolles had four children :

1 Lucius Stillman, born July 6, 1808, at Salem, Mass. [See below.]

2 John Edward, born May 7, 1812, at Salem, Mass ; died of consumption, February 27, 1814.

3 William Carey, born March 8, 1814, at Salem, Mass. [See below.]

4 Lydia Ann, born October 12, 1815, at Salem, Mass. ; died December 24, 1815.

Lucius Stillman, eldest son of Lucius and Lydia (Taber) Bolles, was born July 6, 1808, at Salem, Mass. ; he was a graduate of Brown University in 1828, and received the degree of A. M. in course. He received his degree of M. D. at Harvard College in 1831. Afterwards he studied theology, and was Rector of a Parish in Lynn, Mass., December 4, 1833. He married Sarah Noyes, in Providence, R. I., who died in Philadelphia, Pa., May 20, 1862, at the the residence of her son, Lucius Stillman Bolles, Jr., in the fifty-third year of her age. The Rev. Lucius S. Bolles died at his father's house in Boston, July 23, 1837, of consumption. He was an eloquent and faithful preacher, a loving and devoted son, husband and father. He was buried in the family lot at Mount Auburn. The children of the Rev. Lucius Stillman and Sarah (Noyes) Bolles, were :

1 Nicholas Brown, born February 20, 1835; died September 22,
  1863, of consumption, in Providence, R. I., and was buried
  in Swan Point Cemetery. He graduated at Brown University in 1856; he was a clerk in a Providence banking house
  three or four years.

2 Lucius Stillman, Jr., } born April 21, 1837.
3 John Noyes,

John Noyes died July 12, 1838. Lucius Stillman, the other
twin, graduated at Brown University, 1859; he received
degree of M. D. in Pennsylvania, 1862; he was a surgeòn in
the Union Army during the War of the Rebellion. He married Gertrude Janney, June 15, 1875, in Philadelphia. They
had one child, Gertrude Janney Bolles, born June 21, 1867,
in Philadelphia. Lucius Stillman Bolles, M. D., died August
15, 1873, aged 36 years.

William Carey, third son of Lucius and Lydia Bolles, was
born at Salem, Mass., March 8, 1814. He was fitted for college, but his parents fearing that his health would be affected
by close application to study, sent him to Boston to engage
in mercantile pursuits. He had great musical taste and ability; he played the organ and piano, and had a good tenor
voice. He was baptized July 3, 1831, in Boston; confirmed
in St. James', Roxbury, Mass., by the Right Rev. Manton
Eastburn. He was a sincere and earnest Christian. He
married Frances Mary, daughter of Frances Taber (Allen)
and Jesse Denison Smith, November 22, 1841. He died in
Pomfret, Conn., at 5 P. M., Friday, November 23, 1855, of
consumption, having been sick for many months. His funeral was at his home on Sunday, the Rev. James Morton
officiating, and on Monday, at St. Paul's, Boston, the Rev.
A. H. Vinton, D. D., read the Service. He was buried in his
lot on Fir Avenue, Mount Auburn, with his parents, and
his brother, the Rev. Lucius S. Bolles.

Frances Amelia, only child of William Carey and Frances
Mary Bolles, was born at Boston, Mass., at half-past four, on
Saturday morning, January 27, 1844; she was baptized by

the Rev. Alexander H. Vinton, in St. Paul's Church, of which he was Rector, June 29, 1844. Her great-aunt, Amelia Allen, and her parents were the sponsors. She was confirmed in St. Paul's, Syracuse, N. Y., by the Right Rev. William Heathcote DeLancey, Bishop of Western New York, Thursday afternoon, April 9, 1857. She was educated at St. Mary's Hall, Burlington, N. J., and was married February 8, 1865, at noon, in St. Paul's Church, to George Herbert Patterson, LL. B., by the Rector, the Rev. George Morgan Hills, D. D. The church was beautifully dressed with evergreens, as the Christmas decorations were not removed until after the wedding. The bride was dressed in a rich white gros-grain silk, point lace bertha, a gold chain and cross, the gift of Mrs. Hills, the Rector's wife, a long tulle veil, fastened with orange blossoms and lilies of the valley. They had two bridesmaids and two groomsmen. The Rector said, "It was a Holy Wedding."

George Herbert Patterson, LL. B., was the only son of the Rev. Albert Clarke Patterson, (a graduate of Harvard, 1830, and of the Divinity School, 1833) and his wife Juliet C. (Rathbone) Patterson, and was born at Buffalo, N. Y., December 26, 1836; he was baptized in Trinity Church, by the Rev. Dr. Watson, and confirmed in May, 1859, by the Right Rev. Bishop Spencer, of Madras, in the English Chapel, Rue Marboeuf, Paris, France. He graduated at Hobart College in 1858, and took the Master's degree in 1861. He spent the year after he graduated in travelling in Europe. On his return he went to the Harvard Law School, at Cambridge, Mass., where he received his degree of LL. B. in 1863. He practiced law in Boston till March 1, 1866, when he became Head Master at St. Mark's School, Southborough, Mass., where he remained until March, 1869. In September following, he was elected as Vice-President and subsequently made President of De Veaux College, Suspension Bridge, N. Y. He was there twelve years, resigning July, 1881. He was ordained Deacon in St. Paul's Cathedral, Buffalo, N. Y., on

the third Sunday after Easter (May 8,) 1870, by the Right
Rev. Arthur Cleveland Coxe, Bishop of Western New York.
He was advanced to the Priesthood December 21, 1877, the
Feast of St. Thomas, by the same Bishop, and in the same
Cathedral.

The Rev. Mr. Patterson was Rector of the Berkeley School,
in Providence, R. I., from September, 1883, for five years.
Since August, 1887, he has been Rector of St. Mary's
Church, South Portsmouth, and Holy Cross Chapel, Middletown, R. I.

Frances Amelia (Bolles) wife of the Rev. George Herbert
Patterson, died at South Portsmouth, in St. Mary's Parsonage,
October 16, 1887, aged 43 years, 8 months and 20 days.   She
left us for Paradise about half-past ten, on Sunday morning ;
the funeral service was held at St. Mary's Church, at 8
o'clock, A. M., October 19, 1887, the Rev. George McClellan
Fiske, D. D., Rector of St. Stephen's, Providence, the Rev.
Charles G. Gilliat, Ph. D., and the Rev. Robert B. Peet, taking part in the services.   She was carried to Mount Auburn
and laid in the Bolles lot, Fir Avenue, with her baby and her
sainted father and grand-parents.   The Rev. George S. Pine
said the Committal service at her grave.   She was a devoted
daughter and wife, a loving and faithful mother, and a sincere
Christian.

The following Obituary was written by the Rev. George
Morgan Hills, D. D., her Rector in Syracuse, N. Y., for "The
Churchman " : —

Entered into life eternal, October 16, 1887, at St. Mary's Parsonage, South Portsmouth, R. I., Frances Amelia, wife of the Rev.
George Herbert Patterson, aged 43 years.   Ancestral piety and
excellence went to the making of this good woman.   She seems to
have entered this world sanctified.   At any rate, from the second
life which she received at the Font, there was a continual unfolding
of dispositions and graces which are rarely seen in such complete-
ness.   Goodness was the predominant element in her character, as
well as the chief means for attracting and retaining friendships.

Combine the best qualities of a woman, — daughter, wife and mother, — and you have her depicted. The powers of her mind were commensurate with those of her heart. Tasks which discouraged men, she quietly undertook and did. Her life was its own commendation. Its faithful narration would be its ample eulogy. Her last months of weary waiting were passed with unmurmuring patience, and she entered into "the rest that remaineth," hearing hymns, — the tearless trust and serenity of her departure rounding the rewards of a well-spent life.

"Her children arise up and call her blessed; her husband also, and he praiseth her."

The children of Frances Amelia (Bolles) and Rev. George Herbert Patterson, were as follows :

1 Juliet Clary, born July 27, 1867, at Southborough, Mass. She was baptized by her grandfather, the Rev. Albert Clarke Patterson, in St. Mark's Church, Southborough, October 21, 1867 ; her sponsors were the Right Rev. Henry Adams Neely, D. D., Bishop of Maine, Jane Dows and Annie L. Jones. She was confirmed May 16, 1881, in St. Ambrose Chapel, De Veaux College, by the Right Rev. Arthur Cleveland Coxe, D. D.

2 George Herbert, Jr., born May 11, 1869, at his grandfather's, on Union Terrace, Forest Hills, Mass.; he was baptized July 4, 1869, in St. James' Church (Roxbury), Boston, Mass., by his grandfather, the Rev. Albert Clarke Patterson. His sponsors were the Rev. James A. Bolles, D. D., the Rev. George S. Converse, D. D., and Mrs. Rosalie Heard; he was confirmed in St. Paul's Cathedral, Buffalo, N. Y., by the Right Rev. Arthur Cleveland Coxe, D. D., LL. D., Bishop of Western New York, April 30, 1882.

3 Arthur Bolles, born March 22, 1871, at De Veaux College, Suspension Bridge, N. Y. He was baptized by his father, in St. Ambrose's Chapel, May 1, 1871 (St. Philip and St. James' Day). His sponsors were M. Bainbridge Folwell, M. D., Mr. George F. Lee, and Mrs. Fay Ford Adams ; he was confirmed April 30, 1882, at the same time with his brother George Herbert. They received their first Communion May 18, 1882, in St. Paul's Cathedral, Buffalo, N. Y.

4 Mary Frances, born December 16, 1872, at De Veaux College, Suspension Bridge, N. Y. She was baptized by her father in St. Ambrose's Chapel, February 24, 1873 (St. Matthias' Day); her sponsors were the Rev. James Van Voast, Mrs. Edmund S. Wheeler and Mary Eliza Porter; she was confirmed by the Right Rev. Thomas March Clark, in St. Stephen's Church, Providence, R. I., Ascension Day, 1884.

5 Edith Clarke, born January 20, 1876, at one-quarter before 12, P. M., at Suspension Bridge, N. Y.; baptized by her father in St. Ambrose's Chapel, February 24, 1876 (St. Matthias' Day); her sponsors were the Rev. Walter North, Mary F. Rathbone and Charlotte W. Wheeler. She was confirmed by the Right Rev. Thomas March Clark, D. D., Bishop of Rhode Island, in St. Mary's Church, South Portsmouth, R. I., May 12, 1889, and received her first Communion May 19, 1889 (the fourth Sunday after Easter).

6 Ethel Adams, born September 19, 1878, at Suspension Bridge, N. Y.; she was baptized by her father in St. Ambrose's Chapel, November 3, 1878; her sponsors were George F. Kelley, Madelaine F. Pollock (M. Celeste Rathbone, proxy) and Elizabeth J. Townsend.

7 Ruth Allen, born April 18, 1881, at Suspension Bridge, N. Y.; she was baptized by her father in St. Ambrose's Chapel, June 11, 1881 (St. Barnabas' Day); her sponsors were the Rev. M. C. Hyde, Bessie B. Bird and Sarah C. Very; she died at half-past six, P. M., February 24, 1889 (St. Matthias' Day), at St. Mary's Parsonage, South Portsmouth, R. I., and was buried February 27, 1889, at Mount Auburn, Cambridge, beside her mother and brother; the Rev. Geo. S. Pine read the Committal service. The funeral was at St. Mary's Church, South Portsmouth, R. I. She was a lovely child and a sweet singer.

8 Henry Rathbone, born July 7, 1883, at Rose Cottage (Roxbury), Boston, Mass.; he was baptized by his father in St. Stephen's Church, Providence, R. I., September 29, 1883 (Feast of St. Michael and All Angels); his sponsors were the Rev. William F. Cheney, the Rev. George S. Pine and Mary B. Wheeler.

9 William Carey, born January 27, 1886, at Providence, R. I.; he lived but two hours, and died January 28, 1886; he was buried in the Bolles lot, Fir Avenue, Mount Auburn Cemetery, Cambridge, Mass.

THE STODDARD FAMILY.

Prentice Samuel, son of Vine and Sabria (Avery) Stoddard (see page 58), was born at North Groton, Conn., June 20, 1803. His mother (the first wife of Vine Stoddard) was the daughter of Thomas and Hannah (Smith) Avery. She was born September 10, 1779, and died August 7, 1803. Prentice Samuel was only 7 weeks old, and his mother 24 years and 7 months, when she died.

Vine and Sabria (Avery) Stoddard had two children, Prentice Samuel, above, and Harriet, who was born February 27, 1802; she was married to Sidney Morgan (son of Theophilus), February 27, 1823, who was born August 30, 1800, and died at Salem, Conn., March 26, 1870. Harriet (Stoddard) and Sidney Morgan had five children :

1 Theophilus, born December 27, 1823; married Emily W. Brumley, September 22, 1851.
2 John Wesley, born January 19, 1826; married Lucretia P. Loomis, February 23, 1851; they have one child, a daughter. He is a merchant.
3 Enoch Sidney, born April 3, 1828; married Mary H. Avery, April 6, 1854. They have no children.
4 Albert Hinckley, born October 27, 1833; unmarried.
5 Alva, born August 3, 1840; married Sarah E. Bailey, December 3, 1865. They have no children.

Prentice Samuel, only son of Vine and Sabria (Avery) Stoddard, was a clerk in Joseph Bolles' store in New London for several years; he went from there to Springfield, Mass., with his step-brother, Erastus T. Smith, and was a clerk in his employ; they went to Rochester, N. Y., together, and Mr. Stoddard was Assistant Postmaster there three years.

He married Sarah Ann Osborn, at Homer, N. Y., August
30, 1830, who was born February 12, 1810, at Homer; she
died of consumption, October 18, 1853, at Syracuse, N. Y.,
aged 43 years, 8 months, and 6 days.   After his marriage he
resided in Rochester, where he had one of the largest book-
stores in Western New York.   His health failing, he sold
out, and went to Homer, N. Y.   In 1844 he established a
bookstore in Syracuse, N. Y.; while in that business he
became agent for Livingstone & Wells (Express Company),
and also for two insurance companies; he then sold his book
business, and was an agent for fifteen insurance companies
—two Life, one Marine, and twelve Fire—and did a large
business.   The children of Prentice Samuel and Sarah Ann
(Osborn) Stoddard were:

1 Julia Amelia, born May 19, 1832; died February 11, 1857, of
   consumption, at Syracuse.
2 William Osborn, born September 24, 1835, at Homer, N. Y.;
   married July 25, 1870.   [See below.]
3 Sarah Catharine, born October 9, 1837, at Homer; she was
   married July 5, 1871.   [See below.]
4 Henry Prentice, born August 7, 1840, at Homer; died August
   16, 1867, at New London, Conn.
5 Charles Edward, born November 8, 1842, at Homer; married,
   November 10, 1863, A. Malinda Gilbert, in the 1st Ward
   Presbyterian Church, Syracuse, the Rev. L. H. Reid officiating.
6 John Vine, born June 17, 1845, at Homer; died February 7,
   1879, at Brooklyn, N. Y.

In 1856 Prentice Samuel Stoddard married a second time.
His wife, Frances Mary (Smith-Bolles), was the daughter of
Capt. Jesse Denison and Frances Taber (Allen) Smith, and
widow of William Carey Bolles.   They were married by the
Rev. James Morton, in Christ Church, Pomfret, Conn., September 18, 1856, and went to Syracuse to reside.   In September, 1865, Mr. Stoddard gave up his agencies at Syracuse, and

Rose Cottage, 8 Montrose Street, Boston. Built in 1845.

moved to Boston. In October following he went into the office of Cowles, Brown & Co., and was with them a number of years. Afterwards he was a broker, and had a desk in the office of Freeman & Vinton, remaining there until his last sickness. They were noble men, and true friends to him and his. Mr. Stoddard was a Master Mason, and helped lay the corner-stone of Groton Monument, Connecticut. He was confirmed by the Right Rev. William Heathcote Delancey, S. T. D., in St. Paul's Church, Syracuse, N. Y., March 30, 1858; the Rev. George Morgan Hills, D. D., was Rector of St. Paul's at that time. He died at Rose Cottage, 8 Montrose Street (Roxbury District), Boston, Mass., February 8, 1885, aged 81 years, 7 months, and 19 days. His funeral was attended at the Church of the Messiah, Boston (of which he was a member); the Rev. Henry F. Allen, Rector, and the Rev. George S. Converse, D. D., officiated. At the close of the service, the Rev. George Herbert Patterson went with his remains to Syracuse, N. Y., where he was buried beside his first wife and three of their children, the Rev. Joseph N. Clarke, D. D., saying the Committal service at his grave. Mr. Stoddard was a gentleman who was highly esteemed, and a truly honest man.

William Osborn, son of Prentice L. and Sarah Ann (Osborn) Stoddard, was born in Homer, N. Y., September 24, 1835. He lived in Syracuse, where he fitted for college, and entered Rochester University in 1854; he was editor of the "Central Illinois Gazette" from 1858 to 1861. He was private secretary to President Lincoln from April 1, 1861, to September 24, 1864; he served three months as a volunteer (April, May and June) in 1861; he was Grand Corresponding Secretary of the Union League of America in 1862, 1863 and 1864; United States Marshal of the Eastern District of Arkansas, from September, 1864, to the Spring of 1866. He is the author of "The Life of Abraham Lincoln," and of several other Presidents, and of "Dab Kinzer" and other books for boys. He married, July 25, 1870, in New York City, the

Rev. J. Ryland Kendrick, D. D., officiating, Susan Eagleson Cooper. Their children were :

1 Mabel Cooper, born September 17, 1871, in New York.
2 William Osborn, born March 5, 1873, in New York.
3 Sarah Osborn, born September 28, 1874, in New York.
4 Henry Lincoln, born March 19, 1876, in New York City; died May 4, 1876.
5 Margaret Eagleson ("Daisy"), born August 8, 1877.
6 Guy Avery, born October 12, 1881 : died the same day.
7 Ralph Prentice, born at 7 P. M., August 30, 1887, at Hempstead, Long Island, N. Y.

Mrs. Susan Eagleson (Cooper) Stoddard, was born April 10, 1845, in New York City. She was the daughter of James and Susan Eagleson Cooper.

Sarah Catharine, daughter of Prentice Samuel and Sarah Ann (Osborn) Stoddard, was born at Homer, N. Y., October 9, 1837. She was married July 5, 1871, to James Andrew Gibson, at Brownsville, Texas. They had two children :

1 Henry Stoddard, born February 27, 1873, in Chciago, Ill.
2 James Andrew, born July 9, 1874, in Chicago, Ill. They reside in Syracuse, N. Y.

NATHANIEL ALLEN.

ELIZABETH ALLEN.

WE now return to the descendants of Thomas and Amelia (Taber) Allen. (See pages 36, 37.)

Nathaniel, fifth son of Thomas and Amelia (Taber) Allen, and their seventh child, was born at the home of his grandfather, Pardon Taber, at New London (Great Neck), June 23, 1791. He was baptized in his infancy. At the age of fifteen years he went to Cheshire Academy, and fitted for Yale College, New Haven, Conn., where he graduated September, 1813. Dr. Dwight was then the President, and Nathaniel was much attached to him. He studied medicine, and received his degree of M. D. from the College of Physicians and Surgeons, New York City, in 1817. He was for a time Principal of the Female Academy, New London, Conn. In 1817 Dr. Allen went to Claiborne, Alabama, and was successful as a physician. Here he opened a store, where he sold drugs and dry goods. In June, 1821, he married Martha Helen Foster (daughter of the Rev. Mr. Foster, of Columbia, S. C.), in Claiborne, Ala., the Rev. Mr. Rivers officiating. She was born January 12, 1795, in Columbia, S. C., and her sister, Jane Cellina, who was afterwards married to Henry Nelson Allen (brother of Nathaniel), was born in the same town. Their mother's maiden name was Gadsden. Their only brother was named Gadsden Foster. They were relatives of the Right Rev. Christopher Edwards Gadsden, fourth Bishop of South Carolina.

Dr. Nathaniel Allen died of bilious fever, contracted while visiting his patients, at Claiborne, Ala., August 5, 1822, aged 31 years, 1 month, and 13 days. His widow, Martha Helen Allen, was married, January 26, 1831, to Edward L. Smith, son of Edward and Elizabeth (Grant) Smith, in Claiborne, Ala. He was a merchant in that place, and was born in Stonington, Conn., June 29, 1794. He died January 26, 1873, aged 78 years, 5 months, and 4 days, at the residence of Dr. John Patterson Barnes, in Mobile, whose wife was a niece of Mrs. M. H. (Allen) Smith and Dr. Nathaniel Allen. Her maiden name was Martha Amelia Allen. Mrs. Martha Helen (Allen) Smith died May 15, 1857, aged 62 years, 4 months, and 3 days. Mr. and Mrs. Smith were both buried in Dr. Barnes' lot, in Magnolia Cemetery, Mobile, Ala.

George, the sixth son of Thomas and Amelia (Taber) Allen, was born on Fisher's Island, N. Y., September 21, 1793. He was christened in his infancy by the Right Rev. Samuel Seabury, first Bishop of Connecticut, who also baptized his mother, Amelia (Taber) Allen. He was educated at Cheshire Academy, Connecticut. When very young he went West, first to Illinois, and afterwards to Matamoras, Texas, where he was a merchant. His store, with its contents, was burned, and he then moved to Mexico, and lived in or near the City of Mexico for four years ; he subsequently returned, and settled in Illinois Town, now East St. Louis, where he married, March 19, 1837, Sarah, daughter of Nicodemus and Mary (Homan) Burch, who were born in Virginia,— Mrs. Burch, May 24, 1786, in Loudon County. Mr. and Mrs. Burch were married in Amherst County, Va., in 1804. Nicodemus Burch was born June 8, 1783, and died March 22, 1837, in Waterloo, Ill. His widow died October 1, 1872, in Quincy, Iowa.

Sarah Burch, wife of George Allen, was born in Warren County, Ky., March 5, 1818, and is now living (1891), in Iowa. George Allen died in St. Louis, Mo., December 22, 1844, aged 51 years, 3 months, and 1 day. The children of George and Sarah (Burch) Allen were :

1 Sarah Amelia, born February 27, 1838, at East St. Louis ; she was married April 23, 1864. [See below.]

2 Samuel Nathaniel, born November 22, 1839, at Mount Pleasant, Ill.; died February 22, 1845.

3 Mary Frances, born December 4, 1841, at Waterloo, Ill. ; she was married January 26, 1870. [See below.]

4 Jane Elizabeth, born December 12, 1843, at Waterloo, Ill. ; she was married May 24, 1866. [See below.]

Sarah Amelia, eldest daughter of George and Sarah (Burch) Allen, was born in East St. Louis, Ill., February 27, 1838. She was educated at Jacksonville Academy, Illinois. She was married at Annapolis, Md., April 23, 1864, by the Rev. C. H. Henries, Chaplain in the United States Navy, to Eben Whitney, son of Bennett and Susan (Curtis) Whitney, who were natives of Suffield, Conn. Eben Whitney was born October 22, 1837, in Bridgeport, Conn. He was Captain in the 30th S. C. T., from February, 1864, to December, 1865. He is at present a postal clerk in the railway service, from New York to Philadelphia, on the Pennsylvania Railroad. They have only one child, Bessie Winifred, who was born at Astoria, Long Island, N. Y., January 1, 1875.

Mary Frances, second daughter of George and Sarah (Burch) Allen, was born at Waterloo, Ill., December 4, 1841. She was married by the Rev. William Henderson, Rector of St. John's Church, Keokuk, Ia., January 26, 1870, to Charles William Tracy, who was born in New York City, May 13, 1833. He was a Major in the Army during the Civil War, and is now a civil engineer. They have one child, Charles Alexander, born October 24, 1870, in Marshalltown, Ia.

Jane Elizabeth, youngest daughter of George and Sarah (Burch) Allen, was born at Waterloo, Ill., December 12, 1843 ; she was married by the Rev. E. H. Warring, in Keokuk, Ia., May 24, 1866, to William Bixler, who was born January 22, 1837, in Rogersville, Tuscarawas County, O. Mr. Bixler served several years in an Iowa Regiment during the Civil War. He is a farmer. They have one child, Frank Allen, who was born in Quincy, Ia., October 24, 1867.

John Allen, tenth child of Thomas and Amelia (Taber) Allen, was born on Fisher's Island, N. Y., May 18, 1797. He was baptized in his infancy by the Rev. Charles Seabury, Rector of St. James' Church, in New London, Conn. He married Lucy Johnson, at Albany, N. Y., October 18, 1818. She was born in Groton, Conn. After their marriage they lived in Wolcott, N. Y., until the spring of 1820, when they moved to Pomfret, Conn., and lived on the Nightingale farm. In April, 1824, Mr. Allen's health being impaired, he left home, and went with his brother-in-law, Captain Robert Johnson (who was master of a sealing vessel), to the Southern, or Antarctic, Ocean. Neither captain, crew, passenger or vessel were ever heard from ; it was supposed they were lost among the icebergs. His wife remained at his father's, until it seemed certain he would never return ; she then went with her sister and family, and her three oldest children, to Sinclairville, N. Y., and afterwards moved to Sydney, Fremont County, Ia., where she died October 16, 1857. The children of John and Lucy (Johnson) Allen were :

1 John Wolcott, born July 14, 1819, at Wolcott, N. Y. ; married March 24, 1853. [See below.]
2 Amelia Taber, born August 25, 1820, at Pomfret, Conn. ; she was married in 1836. [See below.]
3 Julia Ann, born November 28, 1821, at Pomfret, Conn. ; she was married October 15, 1848. [See below.]
4 Elizabeth Christophers, born October 1st, 1823, at Pomfret, Conn. ; she was married January 9, 1856. [See below.]

John Wolcott Allen, eldest son of John and Lucy (Johnson) Allen, was born in Wolcott, N. Y., July 14, 1819. He married Mary Ann Pearman, March 4, 1853, at Sydney, Fremont County, Ia. They had two sons born in that town. The oldest, John Howell, was born September 19, 1854; the second, Albert Pearman, was born September 14, 1857. They resided at the West. John Wolcott Allen was a Cavalry officer in the Union Army ; while acting as a scout, in Iowa, his horse was shot under him, and having used his last ammunition, he was taken prisoner. He said, " I had rather die than be a prisoner," when a Rebel officer immediately shot him in the back ; just as he fell some of the Union soldiers met them, and, finding he was dead, buried him and marked his grave. He was killed October 11, 1862, aged 42 years, 9 months, and 3 days. His widow, Mary Ann (Pearman) Allen, was married April 4, 1866, to A. J. Bartlett, as her second husband, and they reside in Iowa.

Amelia Taber, eldest daughter of John and Lucy (Johnson) Allen, was born at Pomfret, Conn., August 25, 1820. She was married in 1836, to Albert Richmond, a lawyer, at Sinclairville, N. Y. They had only one child, Albert, who died in September, 1857, at Sydney, Fremont County, Ia. Amelia Taber (Allen) Richmond died October 17, 1875, at Sinclairville, N. Y.

Julia Ann, second daughter of John and Lucy (Johnson) Allen, was born November 28, 1821, at Pomfret, Conn. She was married October 15, 1848, to Epenetus H. Sears, who was for many years a Judge in Iowa ; he died January 20, 1881. They had no children. Mrs. Julia Ann (Allen) Sears resides at Sydney, Ia.

Elizabeth Christophers, third daughter of John and Lucy (Johnson) Allen, was born at Pomfret, Conn., October 1, 1823. She was married, January 9, 1856, to John McGregor, M. D., by the Rev. Riverius Camp (Rector of Trinity Church, Brooklyn, Conn.), at Thompson, Conn., where he was a practicing physician. Dr. McGregor was born October 10, 1819, at Coventry, Conn. He bore the name of his grandfather, who was one of the lineal descendants of the McGregors of Scotland. Dr. John McGregor died November 4, 1867, in Providence, R. I.

A very full and interesting obituary of Dr. John McGregor was printed soon after his death, filling two columns of a Providence newspaper. He was, as we learn from this, in practice for a time at Phenix, R. I., and subsequently at Thompson, Conn., where he won a high reputation as a surgeon by his successful operations. When the Civil War broke out, he was commissioned as Surgeon of the Third Connecticut Regiment, and was taken prisoner in the first Bull Run battle and sent to Libby Prison, Richmond, and was held for some months ; later in Castle Pinckney, Charleston, when under bombardment from the Union forces. Afterwards he was at Salisbury and Columbia, and again at Richmond until exchanged.

He resided afterwards at Thompson, Conn., and Washington, D. C., but his health, broken by his long confinement, obliged him to relinquish practice and return to Thompson. He was elected Senator from his district, and was chairman of some of the most important committees. " His sense of duty, like his patriotism, was to him a stern and commanding law." He finally located in Providence, R. I., but had been there only fifteen months after his removal to that city when the terrible accident occurred by which he lost his life. While driving, visiting patients, his carriage was overturned by a freight train; he was thrown out, and his arm so seriously injured that it became necessary to amputate it; the doctor did not survive the operation.

Henry Nelson, youngest son (who lived) of Thomas and Amelia (Taber) Allen, was born on Fisher's Island, N. Y., May 27, 1799. He was educated at the Episcopal Academy at Cheshire, Conn. When quite young he went to Claiborne, Ala., where he married, December 10, 1824, Jane Cellina Foster. Miss Foster was born in Columbia, S. C., and was a daughter of a clergyman. Her sister, Martha Helen, married Nathaniel, an elder brother of her husband, in 1821. Jane Cellina Allen died June 3, 1863; Henry Nelson Allen died July 4, 1845, aged 46 years, 1 month, and 7 days. They were both buried in Claiborne, Ala. They had two children, born in Claiborne, of whom the son, Nathaniel, died an infant. Their daughter, Martha Amelia, who was born August 21, 1825, and died October 10, 1886, was married to John Patterson Barnes, M. D., January 15, 1846. Dr. Barnes was City Physician for two years. He died in Mobile, December 1, 1875. He and his wife, Martha Amelia Barnes, were buried in Magnolia Cemetery. Their children were:

1 Henry Allen, born November 23, 1846; killed during the War of the Rebellion.
2 Samuel Thomas, born March 10, 1849.
3 William Edward, born August 2, 1850; died January 21, 1884, in Cameron, Texas.

4 Martha Amelia, born June 26, 1852 ; she was married November 13, 1883. [See below.]

5 John Patterson, born March 5, 1854; married Henrietta Fishbeck ; they had five children. [See below.]

6 Milton Bryan, born November 1, 1885 ; married Lillian Gilbert, and has three children. [See below.]

7 Helen Jane, born August 6, 1857 ; died at Mobile, February 9, 1884.

8 Caroline Olivia, born February 6, 1860.

9 Turner McGavock, born October 12, 1863.

10 James, born April 9, 1866; died April 10, 1866.

Martha Amelia Barnes, fourth child of Dr. John Patterson and Martha Amelia (Allen) Barnes, was born June 26, 1852. She was married November 13, 1883, to James G. Tait, at home, by the Rev. Dr. Burgett, Pastor of Governor Street Presbyterian Church, Mobile, Ala. James G. Tait was born July 4, 1833. He was the son of James Asbury and Martha Goode Tait, and a grandson of Judge J. A. Tait, of Claiborne, Ala. The children of Martha Amelia (Barnes) and James G. Tait were :

1 Helen, born October 11, 1884 ; died April 24, 1885.

2 Albert Lucas, born May 4, 1886.

3 Olivia, born July 22, 1888.

4 Julia, born March 10, 1890.

John Patterson, Jr., son of Dr. John Patterson and Martha Amelia (Allen) Barnes, was born March 5, 1854 ; he married Henrietta Fishbeck, at St. John's Church, Mobile, Ala., the Rev. Asa J. Roberts officiating. Their children were :

1 Walton Webb, born October 21, 1883, at Mobile, Ala.

2 Wilmer Pugh, born December 2, 1885, at Mobile.

3 John Patterson, born March 14, 1888.

4 Albert Doyle and Arthur Kinney, twins, born February 24, 1891. Arthur Doyle died June 21, 1891 ; his disease was cholera infantum ; he was buried the same day in Magnolia Cemetery.

Milton Bryan Barnes, sixth child of Dr. John Patterson and Martha Amelia (Allen) Barnes, was born November 1, 1855. He married Lillian, daughter of Joseph Allen and Morgiana (Whidden) Gilbert, at her mother's house, the Rev. Dr. J. O. Andrews officiating. Their children, all born in Mobile, are:

1 Amelia Allen, born January 27, 1884.
2 Mabel Lillian, born January 14, 1886.
3 Lulu Jeannette, born April 21, 1889.

APPENDIX.

The following Poem, entitled "Evir Allen," is inserted at the suggestion of the late LEWIS D. ALLEN, who has made some comments upon it, which will be found at its close. Mr. Allen was greatly interested in the preparation of the Family Genealogy, and was looking forward to its publication with much pleasure. On the very day of its completion he was called to his reward. He died at Washington, D. C., very suddenly, May 19, 1892, at 2 A. M. His interment was in the family lot at Bellefontaine Cemetery, St. Louis, Mo., where two of his children had been laid. At the time of his death he was the oldest living descendant of Capt. Nathaniel Allen.

EVIR ALLEN.

A POEM.

THOU fairest of the Maids of Morven, young beam of streamy Lutha, come to the help of the aged, come to the help of the distressed. Thy soul is open to pity. Friendship glows on thy tender breast. Ah come and soothe away my woe. Thy words are music to my soul.

Bring me my once loved harp. It hangs long neglected in my hall. The stream of years has borne me away in its course, and rolled away all my bliss. Dim and faded are my eyes; thin strewed with hair my head. Weak is that nervous arm once the terror of foes. Scarce can I grasp my staff, the prop of my trembling limbs.

Lead me to yonder craggy steep. The murmur of the falling streams; the whistling winds rushing through the woods of my hills; the welcome rays of the bounteous sun will soon awake the voice of song in my breast. The thoughts of former years glide over my soul like swift shooting meteors o'er Arden's gloomy vales.

Come, ye friends of my youth, ye soft sounding voices of Cona, bend from your gold tinged clouds, and join me in my song. A mighty blaze is kindled in my soul. I hear a powerful voice. It says, "Seize thy beam of glory, O bard! for thou shalt soon depart.

Soon shall the light of song be faded, soon thy tuneful voice forgotten. "Yes, I obey, O powerful voice, for thou art pleasing to mine ear."

O Evir Allen! thou boast of Erin's maids, thy thoughts come streaming on my soul. Hear, O Malvina! a tale of my youth, the actions of my former days.

Peace reigned over Morven's hills, the shell of joy resounded in our halls. Round the blaze of the oak, sported in festive dance the maids of Morven. They shone like the radiant bow of heaven, when the fiery rays of the setting sun brighten its varied sides. They wooed me to their love, but my heart was silent and cold. Indifference, like a brazen shield, covered my frozen heart.

Fingal saw, he smiled and mildly spake, "My son, the down of youth grows on thy cheek. Thy arm has wielded the spear of war. Foes have felt thy force. Morven's maids are fair, but fairer are the daughters of Erin. Go to thy happy isle; to Branno's grass covered fields. The daughter of my friend deserves thy love. Majestic beauty flows round her as a robe, and innocence as a precious veil heightens her youthful charms. Go take thy arms, and win the lovely fair."

Straight I obeyed. A chosen band followed my steps; we mounted the dark bosomed ship of the king; spread its white sails to the winds, and ploughed through the foam of ocean.

Pleasant shone the fire eyed rell-erin. With joyful songs we cut the liquid way. The moon, regent of the silent night, beamed majestic in the blue vault of heaven, and seemed pleased to bathe her side in the trembling wave. My soul was full of my father's words; a thousand thoughts divided my wavering mind.

Soon as the early beam of morn appeared, we saw the green skirted sides of Erin advancing in the bottom of the sea. White broke the tumbling surges on the coast.

Deep in Larmor's woody bay, we drove our keel to the shore, and gained the lofty beach. I inquired after the generous Branno; a son of Erin led us to his halls, to the banks of the sounding Leno. He said: "Many war-like youth are assembled to gain the dark-haired maid, the beauteous Evir Allen.

Branno will give her to the brave. The conqueror shall bear away the fair. Erin's chiefs dispute the maid, for she is destined for the strong in arms."

These words inflamed my breast, and roused courage in my heart. I clad my limbs in steel. I grasped a shining spear in my hand. Branno saw our approach. He sent the gray-haired Snivan to invite us to his feast, and know the intent of our course. He came with the solemn steps of age, and gravely spake the words of the Chief :

"Whence are these arms of steel ? If friend ye come, Branno invites ye to his halls, for this day the lovely Evir Allen shall bless the warrior's arms, whose lance shall shine victorious in the combat of valour."

"O venerable bard," I said, "peace guides my steps to Branno. My arm is young, and few are my deeds in war, but valour inflames my soul. I am of the race of the brave."

The bard departed. We followed the steps of age, and soon arrived to Branno's halls.

The hero came to meet us. Manly serenity adorned his brow. His open front showed the kindness of his heart. "Welcome," he said, "ye sons of strangers ; welcome to Branno's friendly halls ; partake his shell of joy. Share in the combat of spears. Not unworthy is the prize of valour, the lovely dark-haired maid of Erin ; but strong must be that warrior's hand that conquers Erin's chiefs ; matchless his strength in fight."

"Chief," I replied, "the light of my father's deeds blaze in my soul. Though young, I seek my beam of glory foremost in the ranks of foes ; warrior I can fall, but I shall fall with renown."

"Happy is thy father, O generous youth; more happy the maid of thy love. Thy glory shall surround her with praise, thy valour raise her charms. O were my Evir Allen thy spouse, my years would pass away in joy. Pleased I would descend into the grave ; contented to see the end of my days."

The feast was spread; stately and slow came Evir Allen. A snow white veil covered her blushing face. Her large blue eyes were bent on earth. Dignity flowed round her graceful steps. A shining tear fell glistening on her cheek. She appeared as lovely as the mountain flower when the ruddy beams of the rising sun gleams on its dew-covered sides. Decent she sate. High beat my fluttering heart. Swift through my veins flew my thrilling blood. An unusual weight oppressed my breast. I stood, darkened, in my place. The image of the maid wandered over my troubled soul.

The sprightly harp's melodious voice arose from the strings of the bards. My soul melted away in the sounds, for my heart, like a stream flowed gently away in song. Murmurs soon broke upon our joy. Half unsheathed daggers gleamed. Many a voice was heard abrupt : "Shall the son of the strangers be preferred? Soon shall he be rolled away, like mist, by the rushing breath of the tempest." Sedate I rose, for I despised the boaster's threats. The fair one's eye followed my departure, I heard a smothered sigh burst from her breast.

The horn's harsh sound summoned us to the doubtful strife of spears. Lothmar, fierce hunter of the woody Galmal, first opposed his might. He vainly insulted my youth, but my sword cleft his brazen shield, and cut his ashen lance in twain. Straight I withheld my descending blade ; Lothmar retired confused.

Then rose the red-haired strength of Sulin. Fierce rolled his deep sunk eyes. His shaggy brow stood erect. His face was contracted with scorn. Thrice his spear pierced my buckler. Thrice his sword struck on my helmet. Swift flashes gleamed from our circling blades. The pride of my rage arose. Furious I rushed on the chief, and stretched his bulk on the plain. Groaning he fell to the earth. Lego's shores re-echoed from his fall.

Then advanced Cormac, graceful in glittering arms. No fairer youth was seen on Erin's grassy hills. His age was equal to mine ; his part majestic ; his stature tall and slender, like the young shooting poplar in Lutha's streamy vales ; but sorrow sate upon his brow ; langour reigned on his cheek. My heart inclined to the youth. My sword oft avoided to wound ; often sought to save his days ; but he rushed eager on death. He fell. Blood gushing from his panting breast. Tears flowed streaming from mine eyes. I stretched forth my hand to the chief. I proffered gentle words of peace. Faintly he seized my hand : "Stranger," he said, "I willingly die, for my days were oppressed with woe. Evir Allen rejected my love. She slighted my tender suit. Thou alone deservest the maid, for pity reigns in thy soul, and thou art generous and brave. Tell her I forgive her scorn. Tell her I descend with joy into the grave ; but raise the stone of my praise. Let the maid throw a flower on my tomb, and mingle one tear with my dust ; this is my sole request. This she can grant to my shade."

I would have spoken, but broken sighs issuing from my breast, interrupted my faltering words. I threw my spear aside. I clasped the youth in my arms; but alas! his soul was already departed to the cloudy mansions of his fathers.

Thence thrice I raised my voice, and called the chiefs to combat. Thrice I brandished my spear, and wielded my gleaming sword. No warrior appeared. They declared the force of my arm, and yielded the blue eyed maid.

Three days I remained in Branno's halls. On the fourth he led me to the chamber of the fair. She came forth attended by her maids, graceful in lovely majesty, like the moon, when all the stars confess her sway, and retire respectful and abashed. I laid my sword at her feet. Words of love flowed faltering from my tongue. Gently she gave her hands. Joy seized my enraptured soul. Branno was touched at the sight. He clasped me in his aged arms.

"O wert thou," he said, "the son of my friend, the son of the mighty Fingal, then were my happiness complete."

"I am, I am the son of thy friend," I replied, "Ossian, the son of Fingal," then sank upon his aged breast; our flowing tears mingled together; we remained long clasped in each others' arms.

Such was my youth, O Malvina! but alas, I am now forlorn. Darkness covers my soul; yet the light of song beams at times on my mind; it solaces away my woe.

Bards, prepare my tomb. Lay me by the fair Evir Allen. When the revolving years bring back the mild season of spring to our hills, sing the praise of Cona's bard, of Ossian, the friend of the distressed.

IMPROMPTU, ON THE POEM.

The foregoing epic poem, " Evir Allen," by Baron De Harold, is one of great beauty, and calculated to inspire valour, wisdom, virtue and morality; and illustrates most happily true friendship. Its style is chaste, pure and beautiful; and accords in many points with the principles embodied in the coat of arms and motto of the Allen family.

The subjects of this poem lived in the third century. Fingal's death is stated to have taken place in 286, as we all know; ancient history is involved in much uncertainty as to time and date.

The author of this poem assures the public that the materials were gathered with much assiduity and care, from fragmentary history, songs of old bards, and traditions ; claiming only the embelishments as his own.

The Honorable Henry Grattan, Esq., to whom the Baron dedicated his work, this poem being a part, has said, "the poems it contains are calculated to inspire many virtues ; and are adorned with numerous beauties in poetry and morality, and are illuminated by noble illustrations to the Omnipotent."

This poem differs widely in sentiment from those of the book proper of Ossian by MacPherson.

L. D. ALLEN.

WASHINGTON, D. C., Jan. 7th, 1892.

INDEX.

I. — ALLEN: CHRISTIAN NAMES.

No attempt is made in the following list to distinguish between different individuals having the same Christian name.

II. — ENGLISH ALLENS MENTIONED.

III. — ALLIED FAMILIES.

IV. — FAMILIES ALLIED TO ENGLISH ALLENS.